MAY 1982.

To.

Ann,

WITH BEST WISHES
FOR A VERY HAPPY
BIRTHDAY.

LOVE,

Liam & Tom.

x x x x

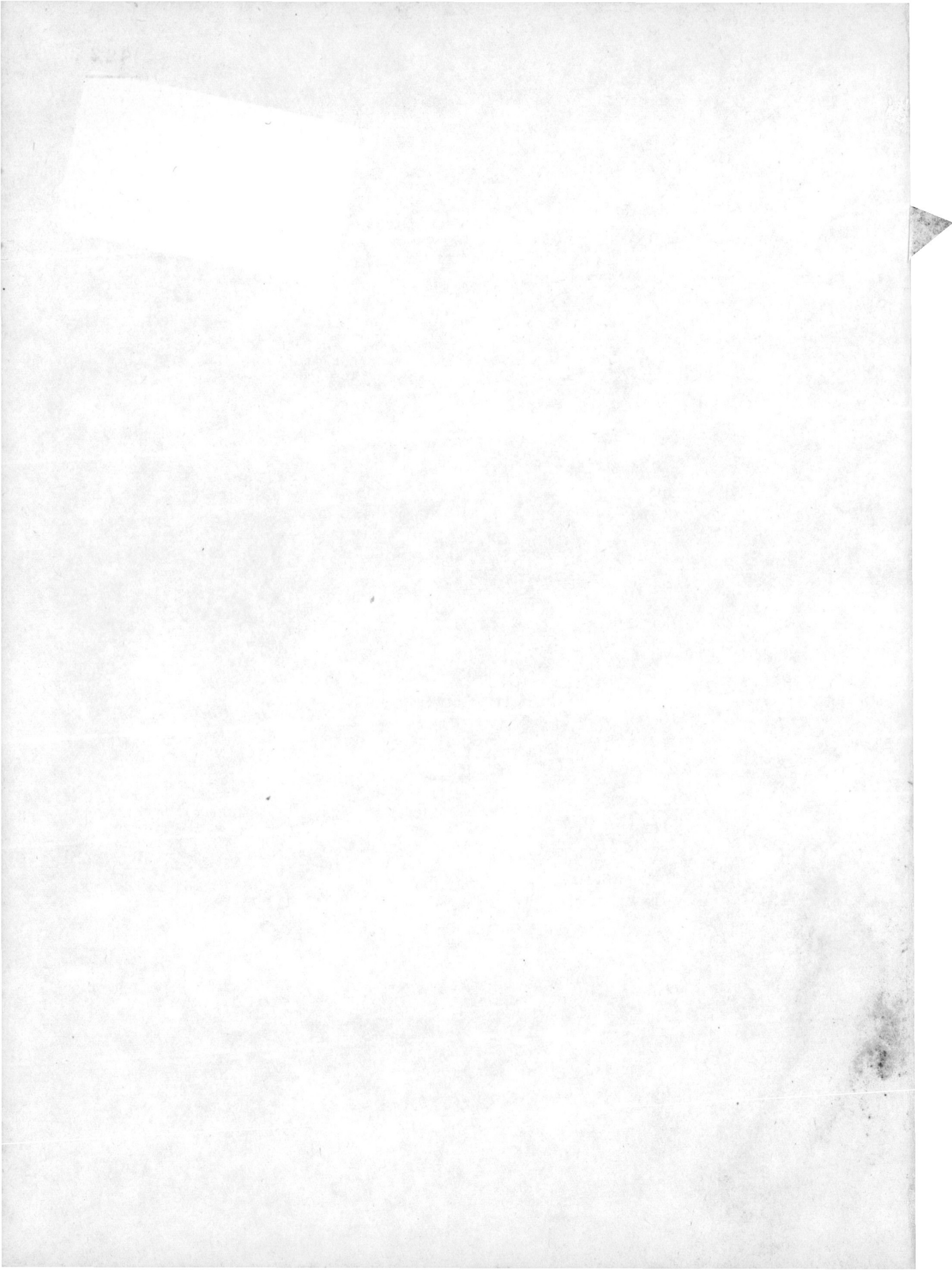

GOLF

Also by Ken Adwick, published by Pelham Books

X-Ray Way to Master Golf
Ken Adwick's Alphabet of Golf

Also in the Pelham Pictorial Sports Instruction Series

Chester Barnes : Table Tennis
Henry Cooper : Boxing
John Dawes : Rugby Union
Richard Hawkey : Squash Rackets
Barry Richards : Cricket
Bob Wilson : Soccer

In preparation

Rachael Heyhoe Flint : Women's Hockey
Jack Karnehm : Understanding Billiards and Snooker
Paul and Sue Whetnall : Badminton

Pelham Pictorial Sports Instruction Series

Ken Adwick
GOLF

edited by James Green
with a foreword by Tony Jacklin, O.B.E.
artwork on illustrations by Ken Adwick

Pelham Books

First published in Great Britain by
PELHAM BOOKS LTD
52 Bedford Square
London WC1B 3EF
1975

ISBN 0 7207 0852 4

Printed in Great Britain by
Fletcher & Son Ltd, Norwich

Contents

Photograph by G. L. Pike

Foreword

The first time I met Ken Adwick was when I had my swing action and putting style analysed by his X-ray process for a colour magazine article. He handed me the pictures on my birthday — and they were not only interesting but proved a good luck charm as during that same week I won my British Open title at Royal Lytham and St. Annes. Since then Ken and I have met on various occasions including the Canadian Open, where we were both competing, and in the United States. That was during the American Open.

Through his books and articles in *Golf World* he has become a foremost golfing teacher known for his detailed knowledge of playing technique. So much so that many tournament stars have sought his advice over the years.

Ken Adwick has made a deep study of every aspect of this great game and I have much pleasure in supporting and unhesitatingly recommending his words of wisdom.

Tony Jacklin, O.B.E.

This book is dedicated to the beginner and club golfer. They are the backbone of the game and the potential champions of tomorrow.

My thanks to James Green for his editorial assistance in the preparation of this book. I also wish to thank those golfers, both amateur and professional, who readily volunteered to allow me to take pictures of their swings for this book.

Preface

So you are thinking of taking up golf.

Here is a book of simple instruction which will not
only serve the beginner but give guidance to players
who have had experience of the game. It will even
help the most advanced golfer if he wants to check back
to the basics of the art.

Virtually all the photographs I have taken myself.

Ken Adwick

List of Illustrations

CHAPTER ONE

Introduction to Golf

Welcome to golf. The day you discover it is sure to be one of the happiest of your life. In my view, shared by many others, golf is the finest game of them all.

Why? It demands mental ability as well as physical skill. It is played in the open air and invariably amid attractive scenery. It is a game you can play and enjoy for a lifetime. You can play it on your own, with a friend or friends, in good weather or bad. And because of the handicapping system the less skilled player still has a real chance of beating an experienced opponent.

You will make friends through golf, and I think it is a fine character builder as a high code of conduct is expected of the player. He is placed on his honour not to cheat or break the rules.

So if you are thinking of trying the game do not hesitate to make a start — although I must warn you that none of us is ever able to say that we have mastered it. It will involve time, practice, intelligence and a measure of dedication, but the rewards eventually more than compensate. In a sense you are not only playing an opponent and the hazards of the course . . . but playing yourself, too. Golf reveals as well as builds character.

You have only yourself to blame should you play badly, and equally you can take quiet pride when you have given of your best and won the day. Most golfers in my experience are modest in victory, and I think there is an interesting point here. With many sports the champions can be certain of performing to their exalted level, but the golfer taking his prize has no certainty of how well he will play the next day.

I have taught professionals at all levels and I have taught the basics of golf to thousands of novices — ranging from the smallest schoolboys to captains of industry. Virtually without exception they all have said they wish they had taken up golf earlier.

What is the best age to start? And how old is too old? In brief, there is no age when you cannot start. But I believe the best age to begin — with any degree of purpose — is around nine to twelve years. Youngsters of that age are natural imitators or mimics and have a gift for copying what they see. They watch a good player swing a club and find little difficulty in swinging something like him and along a correct line.

Yet while the young may take to golf instinctively, it is much better for their long-term development if during their

SHAFT

SOLE
PLATE

TOE

NECK

FACE
INSERT

HEEL

STRING

SHAFT

GRIP

SOLE

HEEL

TOE

GRIP LINES

HOSEL

FERRULE

SHAFT

CAP

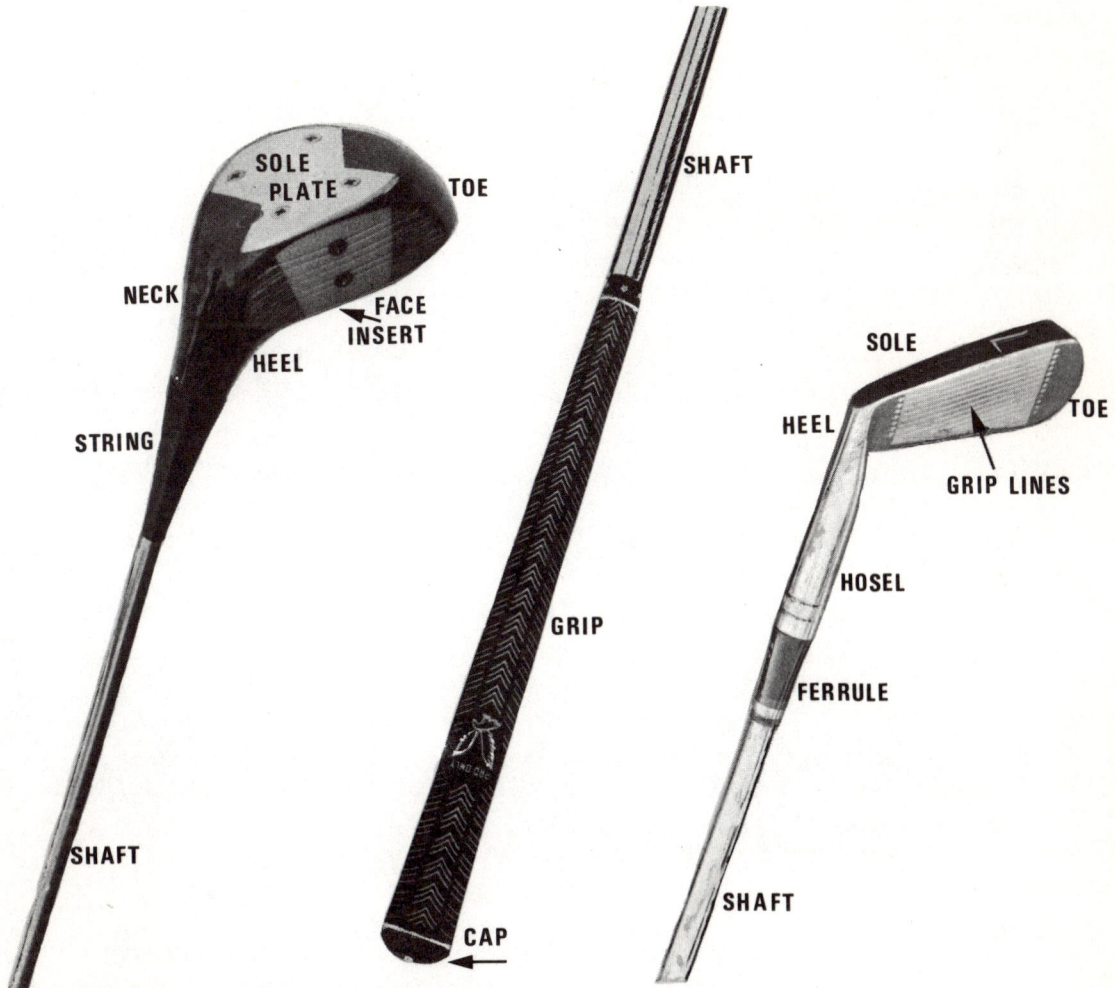

1. Description of wood and iron clubs.

early period they have the benefit of a course of lessons. These can be taken individually or as part of a group. Then the professional is able to ingrain correct habits instead of, at a later date, having to waste time breaking down some bad habits that have been acquired before he can start giving positive instruction.

A lot of parents do not bother to provide expert teaching for their children. Some fathers play the game themselves and think they can teach the rudiments. The expert, they reason, is not needed until the boy or girl knows more about the game. So father and son go out and play together. Dad no doubt has some weaknesses in his game and the boy is invariably guided into the same errors. *I strongly advise any fathers reading this book not to teach their own children.* Encourage them by all means but leave the instruction to your professional.

Golf
WOODS

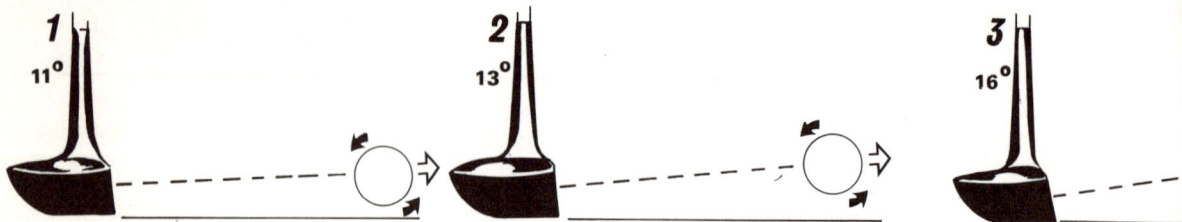

IRONS

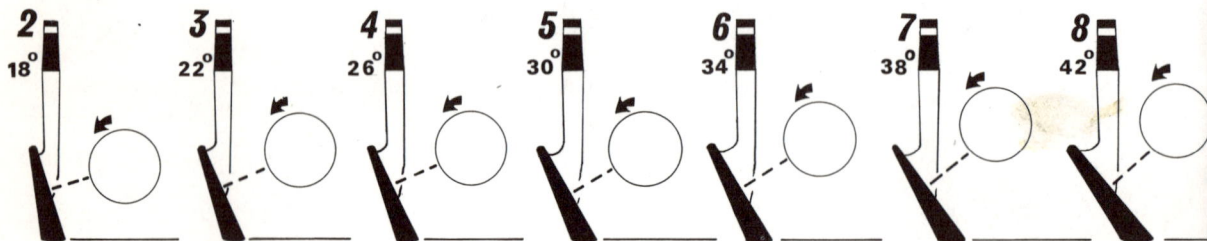

The degrees marked are the general lofts for woods and irons.

Anti-clockwise spin.

2. A complete set of clubs showing the various lofts. The No. 1 wood (or driver), being the longest club in the bag and with the least loft, theoretically produces the lowest trajectory shot and the greatest distance.

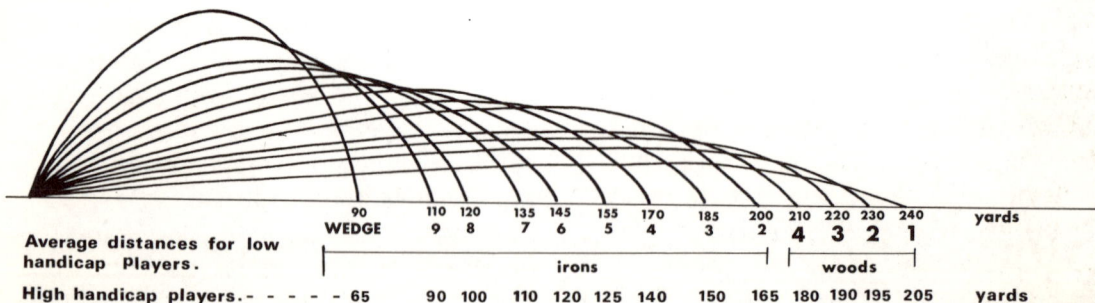

	WEDGE														yards
	90	110	120	135	145	155	170	185	200	210	220	230	240	
		9	8	7	6	5	4	3	2	4	3	2	1	

Average distances for low handicap Players.

irons   woods

High handicap players.- - - - - 65   90 100   110 120 125 140   150   165 180 190 195 205   **yards**

AVERAGE DISTANCES FOR WOODS AND IRONS.

14

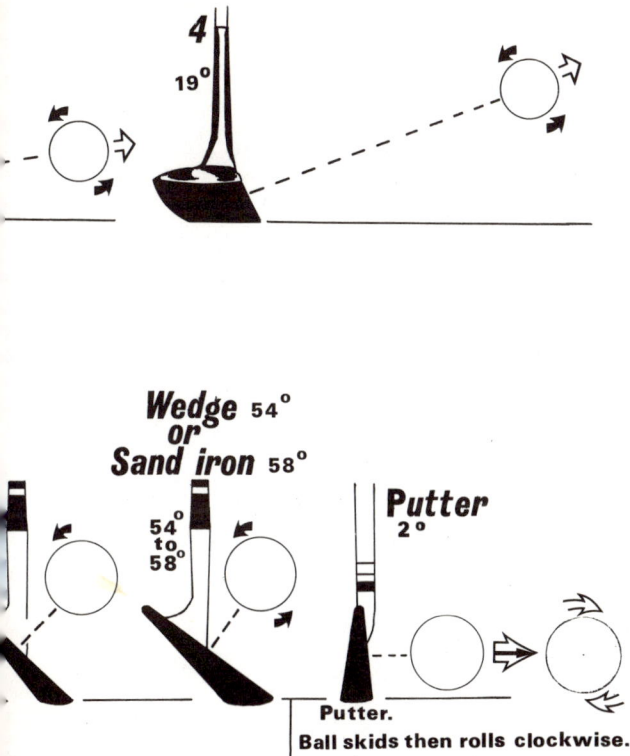

4
19°

Wedge 54°
or
Sand iron 58°

54°
to
58°

Putter
2°

Putter.
Ball skids then rolls clockwise.

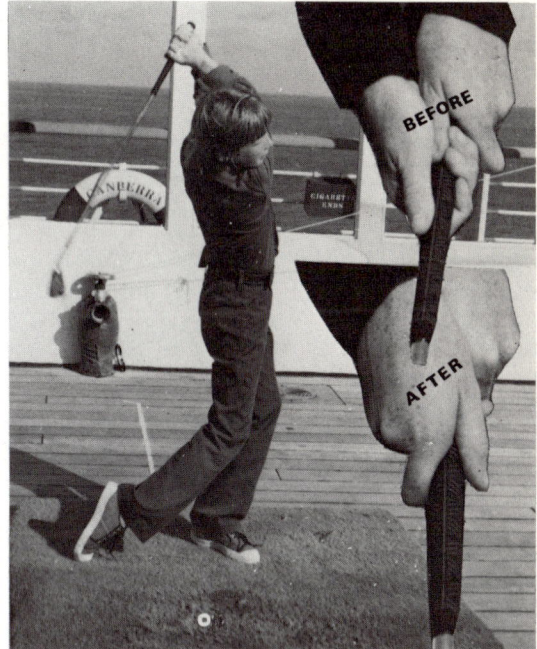

4. *David Morgan, 11-year-old Scot and 16 handicap player (from the Ladies' tees) displays a good follow-through. Before instruction he had a poor grip with both hands too far round to the right. For this reason he found difficulty getting the ball into the air when using his long irons and woods – a common fault. As an over-correction I asked him to adopt the correct hold with his left hand but place his right hand slightly further left than is required, advising him to return it to the correct position after a few weeks of practice.*

Now what about suitable clubs for these nine to twelve year olds? Some fathers cut down their old clubs and pass them on. That is wrong because the clubs are too heavy and the shafts too stiff. When a club is cut down in size the shaft becomes even stiffer. Ideally the boy should use junior clubs or cut down ladies' clubs. At this stage secondhand clubs are quite good enough. Not that the beginner will need any clubs in order to take a lesson. The professional will be happy to loan a suitable club from his secondhand stock.

Just a brief word about the usual categories of beginners. There are four main entry divisions: the very young; teenagers; the 'young marrieds' and rising career men; and senior citizens looking for a new interest (or taking up golf for health reasons) now that they have time to spare.

CHAPTER TWO

The Course and the Handicapping System

A golf course consists of 18 holes (there are some 9-hole courses where you play round twice) and is generally between 5,500 and 7,000 yards in length.

Of the 18 holes the majority – probably about 10 – are what we call par-fours. Then there are 4 short holes, called par-threes, and 4 long holes, called par-fives. The proportions can vary.

Par in each case is the number of shots a good golfer should take to complete that hole. For the example I have just given the par for the whole course is 72 shots. The player who achieves that has played to scratch. If he goes round in 75 then he has 'dropped three shots' or, as they say in television golfing commentaries, is 'three over'. All professionals play off scratch.

The golf handicapping system works

5. *Illustration of a golf hole.*

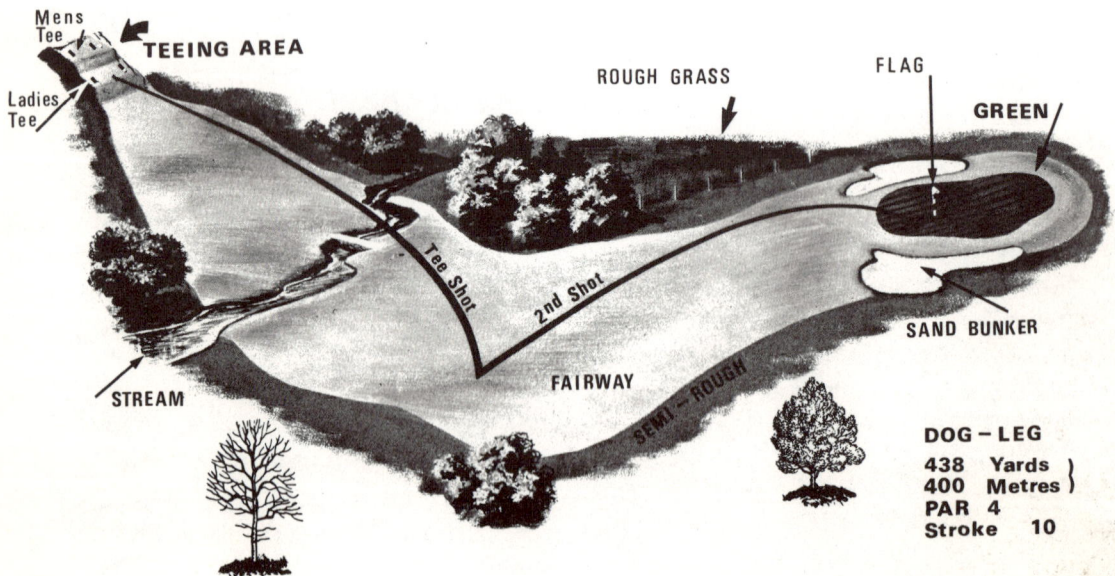

Mens Tee
TEEING AREA
Ladies Tee
ROUGH GRASS
FLAG
GREEN
Tee Shot
2nd Shot
SAND BUNKER
STREAM
FAIRWAY
SEMI – ROUGH

DOG – LEG
438 Yards
400 Metres
PAR 4
Stroke 10

this way : as a newcomer you are given a 'courtesy' handicap of 24. That is the maximum anyone is allowed (except that the ladies' maximum handicap is 36). It means you have 24 shots start when playing against the course.

The man who completes that par-72 course in 80 shots is handicap 8, and the man scoring 92 is handicap 20.

You get your handicap adjusted by putting in score cards for a round or rounds.

I have mentioned par-three, par-four and par-five holes. In each case two of those shots are assumed to be on the putting green. So it follows that on the par-three short holes the player is expected to hit the green with his tee shot, on the par-fours he has a drive and a second shot in order to reach the green, while on the long fives he is allowed a drive, followed by two more shots before reaching the green.

If you hole out in one shot less than par for the hole then you have a 'birdie', while two shots under par is an 'eagle'.

Stroke play is the most usual form of competition and is decided by the number of strokes you have taken to complete 18 holes, less your handicap. For example, 89 minus 12 handicap returns a card of 77. You are playing against the whole field and the lowest net score wins.

In match play you are playing against one particular opponent, or opponents, and scoring is by holes. So if you are four holes ahead walking off the 15th green you have won by 4 and 3. That is, four holes up with three left.

The way handicaps work in match play is that the highest handicap player gets three-quarters of the difference between his handicap and his opponent's.

For example, if your handicap is 12 and the opponent plays off 4 handicap, then the difference is 8. You receive three-quarters of 8, i.e. you are entitled to six strokes. You will take these shots individually where they are indicated on the score card.

In a stapleford competition you receive seven-eighths of your handicap. As with match play you take these shots as they come on the card, except that in stapleford competition you are scoring points — one point for taking one shot over par, two points for a hole in par, three points for a birdie. Should you be lucky enough to score an eagle (two shots under par) you will be awarded four points. A player who scores the lowest at a hole during a medal round and the man who wins a hole in match play has the honour off the next tee (plays his tee shot first) and does so until the position is reversed.

On the course itself there are tee areas used for driving off at each hole, sand and grass bunkers, fairways and rough, natural obstacles such as ditches and trees, and frequently a lake or streams. (See Fig. 5.)

Most important, when on the course never play a shot if there is any danger of reaching the players in front. If by chance a ball is travelling close to other people then always give a loud cry of 'fore'.

Finally, if you are interested in golf never be anxious about asking for guidance from your local golf club secretary or professional. We all had to begin and golf is becoming increasingly a young man's game. Just as long as you learn the etiquette you will soon be welcome.

KNOLE PARK GOLF CLUB
Standard Scratch Score 70

Date **6ᵀᴴ JUNE**
Handicap **15**
Strokes Rec'd **15**

Player **H. ROSE**   Competition **MEDAL**

Markers Score	Hole	Yards	*Metres*	Par	Stroke Index	Player's Score		Marker's Score	Hole	Yards	*Metres*	Par	Stroke Index	Player's Score	
3	1	197	180	3	9	4		3	10	163	149	3	18	3	
4	2	345	315	4	13	5		5	11	426	389	4	2	5	
5	3	403	368	4	5	5		5	12	200	183	3	8	4	
4	4	413	377	4	3	6		3	13	319	292	4	14	4	
3	5	174	159	3	11	3		3	14	438	400	4	4	5	
4	6	418	382	4	1	5		4	15	483	441	5	10	6	
5	7	480	439	5	15	5		3	16	199	182	3	6	4	
2	8	177	162	3	17	4		5	17	502	459	5	16	7	
6	9	512	468	5	7	6		4	18	400	366	4	12	4	
OUT		3119	2850	35		**43**		**IN**		3130	2861	35		**42**	

Player's Signature **H. Rose**

Marker's Signature *[signature]*

	OUT	3119	2850	35	**43**
	TOTAL	6249	5711	70	**85**
	HANDICAP				**15**
	NET SCORE				**70**
	BOGEY RESULT				**—**

KNOLE PARK GOLF CLUB
STABLEFORD CONVERSION TABLE

Strokes will be taken at the allotted holes on the basis of:⅝
SINGLES — ⅞ths of Handicap.
FOURSOMES — ⁷⁄₁₆ths of Combined Handicaps of each side.

SINGLES		FOURSOMES			
Handi-cap	Stroke Allow-ance	Combined Handicaps	Stroke Allow-ance	Combined Handicaps	Stroke Allow-ance
1	1	1	0	25	11
2	2	2	1	26	11
3	3	3	1	27	12
4	4	4	2	28	12
5	4	5	2	29	13
6	5	6	3	30	13
7	6	7	3	31	14
8	7	8	4	32	14
9	8	9	4	33	14
10	9	10	4	34	15
11	10	11	5	35	15
12	11	12	5	36	16
13	11	13	6	37	16
14	12	14	6	38	17
15	13	15	7	39	17
16	14	16	7	40	18
17	15	17	7	41	18
18	16	18	8	42	18
19	17	19	8	43	19
20	18	20	9	44	19
21	18	21	9	45	20
22	19	22	10	46	20
23	20	23	10	47	21
24	21	24	11	48	21

WINTER RULE. When this is in force a ball lying on the fairway or green surround may be lifted, cleaned and placed within six inches but not nearer the hole.

LOCAL RULES

1. **OUT OF BOUNDS**, Penalty — Loss of Stroke and Distance.
   The following are out of bounds:-
   The practice putting green and all paths around the Clubhouse including spur paths if within an area formed by projecting or extending the boundary line.
   Over all walls and fences forming a boundary of the course.
   14th hole. In or over the ditch.
2. Stones in bunkers may be treated as moveable obstructions. Rule 31-1 applies.
3. **ROADS.** A ball resting on a tarmacadamed road must be lifted and dropped not nearer the hole; without penalty.
4. **LIFTING BALL WITHOUT PENALTY**
   A ball may be lifted and dropped not nearer the hole and unless stated otherwise, as near as possible to where it lay.
   (a) If a sucker on a mown fairway.
   (b) If lying in a wheel rut or drain.
   (c) If lying within two clubs' lengths of a tree stump or fallen tree, it may be lifted and dropped not more than two clubs' lengths from where it lay.
   (d) If lying on the metalled cart track crossing the 7th fairway.
   (e) When playing the 17th hole a ball finishing on the metalled cart track running along the side of and crossing the fairway may be lifted and dropped outside or behind the track not nearer the hole without penalty.
5. **LATERAL WATER HAZARD.** The ponds at the 4th, 8th, 9th and 11th holes are deemed to be Lateral Water Hazards.

6. (above) *A marked scorecard for a medal round. The reverse side (below) outlines the local rules for that particular course and shows a handicap conversion table.*

CHAPTER THREE

Introducing the Clubs – Grip

We are allowed up to 14 clubs in a golf bag – not that the novice needs that many. They divide into the woods, the irons and the putter.

The club intended to send the ball the longest distance has the least loft – lack of loft is useful for making the ball fly low. The distance clubs are also longer in shaft length.

Take the woods first. The No. 1, or driver, is the lightest club of all but the most powerful. It is the last club the beginner should use because it is also the most difficult.

The No. 2 wood, or brassie, can be used for driving off the tee or for long fairway shots.

The No. 3 wood, or spoon, and the No. 4 wood can also be taken off the tee, but are essentially for use on the fairway or from light rough.

Now the irons. Although there are Nos. 1- and 2-irons they are for experts and have no real place in the newcomer's bag. Nos. 3- and 4-irons are used for distance and on average are more accurate than woods.

Nos. 5, 6 and 7 are mid-irons and are used for accuracy for the distance required.

The 8- and 9-irons, and wedge, are short-distance precision clubs where pin-splitting is expected. The sand iron is for escaping from bunkers and the putter is used to hole out on the putting green. (See Fig. 2.)

Next we come to the actual use of these clubs. This introduces the vital subjects of grip, stance and swing.

Many an untutored beginner, holding the club wrongly and doing everything instinctively, will claim to have little initial problem in hitting a reasonably straight ball.

I agree. But that good fortune is not going to last and in no time he will start hitting poor shots. You must not be content to adopt your own way. *The basics of grip and stance must be mastered* because your whole swing will follow from these. The approved grip and stance may feel awkward at first but they hold the key to progress.

Unfortunately, the natural way to hit a golf ball is the wrong way. That is why instruction is so very necessary. The untutored will always hit a ball the wrong way – almost to a man they slice (the ball starting straight or left but turning sharply right during flight).

Incidentally, when you do start learning correctly, the best club to take out is a 5-iron. It is a mid-iron, not too long in the shaft and with a good degree of loft. It is a club you can control quite easily.

Now for the hold on the club known as the grip. *The hands are the tools of the brain, whatever they hold they are in command of*, all body movements are responsive to the path on which the clubhead is swung, so it follows that the grip is of paramount importance because the hands are the only link between club and player and as you grip so you will swing. Any change of grip will alter the swing path.

There are three forms of grip. Two of which we can forget because the third, the Vardon grip, is overwhelmingly used and recommended.

By the way, don't let that word 'grip' mislead you. It might be better to think of 'holding' instead. Most amateurs grip far too tightly. We don't want the white of the knuckles showing. When it comes to pressure and 'feel', the first finger and thumb of the right hand and the last three fingers of the left are the ones that matter.

To get the Vardon grip place your left hand on the club with the 'V' shape made by first finger and thumb pointing straight up the shaft at you. This is the view as seen only by the player.

Now place the right hand below the left and move the little finger of the right hand over the first finger of the left. The reason we do that is to reduce some of the power of the right hand and also to give better 'feel'. The 'V' of the right hand should also be pointing up the shaft.

When the club is being held correctly you should be showing two and a half knuckles of the left hand. Show four knuckles and the grip is too strong, show one and the grip is too weak.

You are bound to find this orthodox grip strange at first, but whatever your feelings *persevere with it* and very shortly it will become second nature.

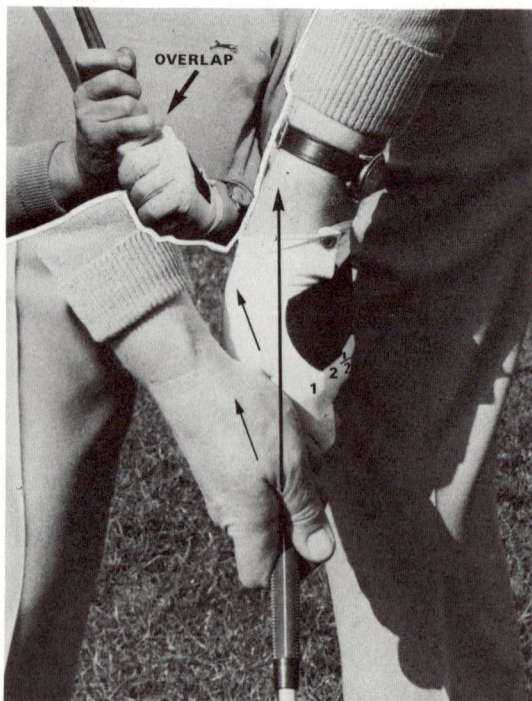

7.   The Vardon Grip. This is the correct way to hold the club. It enables both wrists to hinge correctly through the swing. The inverted 'V's formed by thumb and first finger point between the player's neck and right shoulder – as seen by an onlooker. To the player himself the 'V's will appear to be pointing towards his chin. He will also see two and a half knuckles of his left hand. The insert picture shows this hold from the reverse side with the little finger of the right hand overlapping the first finger of the left. Note the trigger-like position of the first finger of the right hand. This helps to develop clubhead 'feel' during the swing. Virtually all golfers use a specially made left-hand glove which helps to maintain a firm hold, so aiding control.

The Vardon grip works well because the palms of the hands are in direct opposition and can work as one unit.

The biggest fault is generally found in the right hand which has gradually

slipped under the clubshaft because it feels in a more powerful position there. So it is. But it is wrong because it will overpower the left hand which is trying to control the clubhead through the shot.

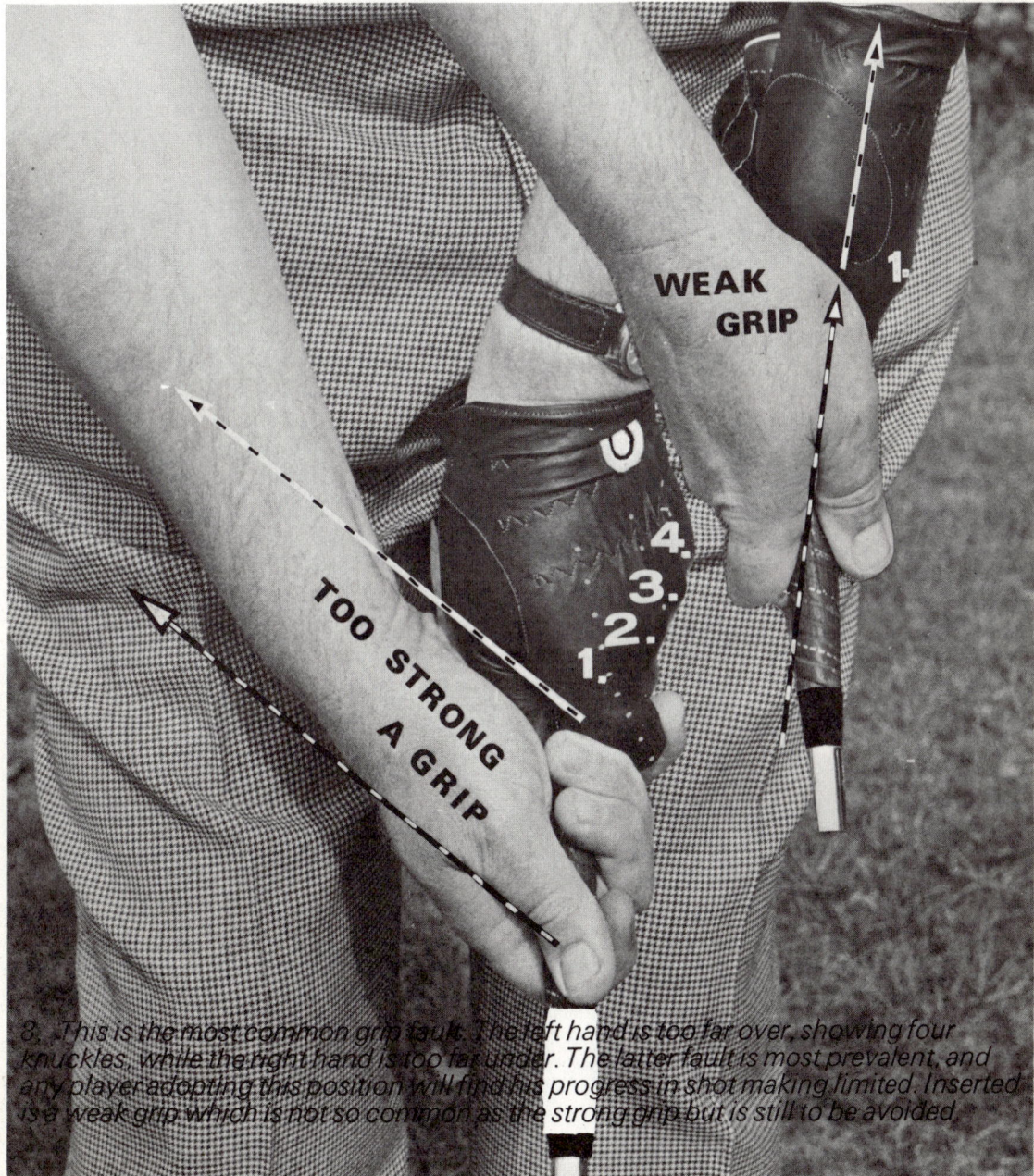

8. This is the most common grip fault. The left hand is too far over, showing four knuckles, while the right hand is too far under. The latter fault is most prevalent, and any player adopting this position will find his progress in shot making limited. Inserted is a weak grip which is not so common as the strong grip but is still to be avoided.

Golf

We do not want a vice-like grip even though it may seem that by gripping tight the ball will be given a resounding whack. Just hold the club as if you were giving a firm handshake. If you hold on too tight, other muscles tighten up as well and freedom of swing disappears. Instead of swinging the club, the club swings you.

A light grip is even preferable to a vice-like one. But watch out for the danger of the fingers of the left hand opening at the top of the backswing into what is known as a piccolo grip. Keep those fingers firm and round the shaft.

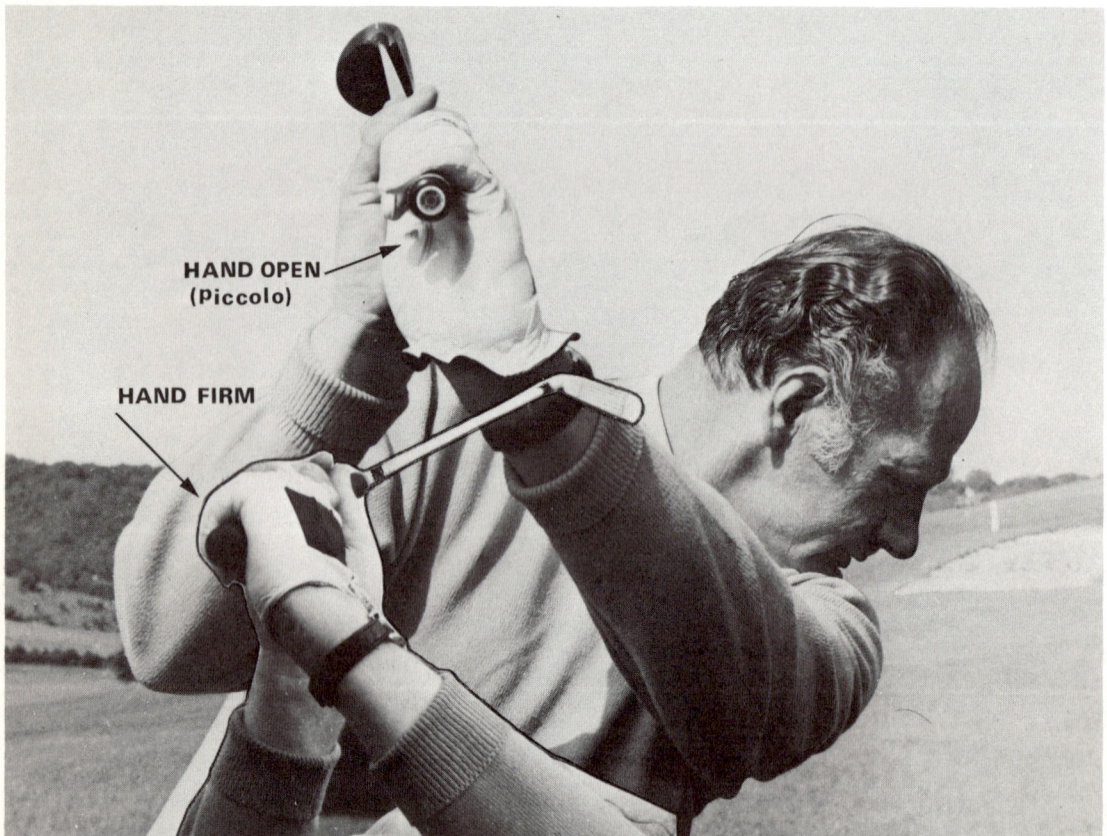

HAND OPEN (Piccolo)

HAND FIRM

9. *A slack grip results in poor control. The left hand will usually open at the top of the backswing and point away from the intended line of flight, with the clubface open. It can also cause overswinging and throwing the clubhead from the top of the swing. This is known as a piccolo grip. The inserted picture shows the left-hand in control with the right wrist under the shaft, keeping the clubface square.*

CHAPTER FOUR

Stance

Having learned the right way to hold a club, the next question is how to address the ball. In other words, stance. This again is 100 per cent important.

The correct stance gives a feeling of balance and freedom when swinging the club and allows the clubface to be returned squarely to the back of the ball.

TARGET LINE

10. *It is essential to wear studded shoes when playing in order to maintain good anchorage. Lee Trevino is pictured here at practice during the U.S. Championship wearing unstudded boots while waiting for his caddie to bring his golf shoes.*

23

Golf

The feet should be placed as wide apart as your shoulders and the toes can be turned out a little. The knees should be flexed a bit. Get the impression that you are about to sit down. Flexing the knees reduces tension and helps spread the weight evenly on both feet.

Never have the weight on the balls of the feet, as that tips you forward too much. Better to feel the weight is slightly backwards on the heels.

If your feet are too far apart then you introduce tension and will have extra difficulty in turning correctly. But when the feet are too close there is a feeling of insecurity.

11. The great Ben Hogan. Seldom photographed, he is shown here at perfect address position – knees flexed, toes turned out a little, shoulders and hips square to line of flight, ball positioned just inside the left heel, arms and clubshaft forming a perfect letter 'Y', and a grip that is absolute perfection.

STANCE TOO WIDE   CORRECT

12. 11-year-old Jonathan Drummond had his feet too wide apart which restricted responsive body movements when swinging the clubhead. The narrower stance in the right-hand picture is the form to adopt.

The clubhead is positioned squarely behind the ball with the hands opposite the ball – i.e. a little ahead of the clubface, but never ahead of the ball itself.

DRIVER   5 IRON

13. The clubface must be squarely placed behind the ball with the hands opposite the ball. Now the hands will be just ahead of the clubface. In general, for the woods, the ball is lined up a few inches inside the left heel. For the irons, position yourself so that the ball will be back more towards the middle of the feet, by which time the 9-iron or wedge is being used.

Golf

Then the pupil will ask 'How do I know whether I am standing too near or too far ?' Obviously the longer the club the further away from the ball we stand. The common fault among handicap players is to stand too far from the ball. They feel this is a powerful position but in reality it is weaker.

There is a simple way to find your correct position : stand upright holding the club horizontally out in front of you. Then lower the club to the ground by bending *your back only*. But do not lower your club, hands and arms independently of your body because you are not only trying to find your correct distance but also your correct posture.

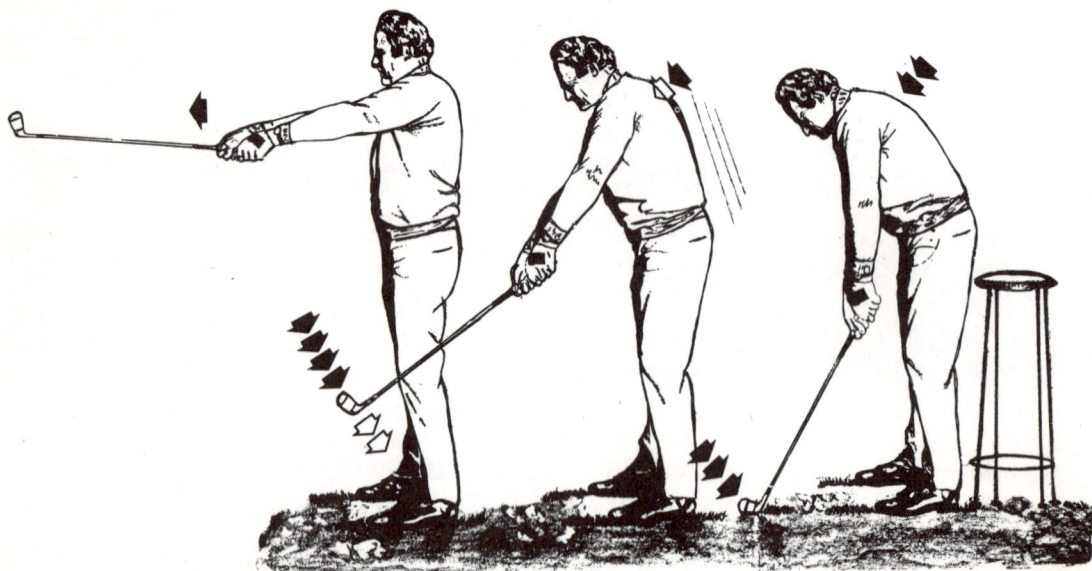

14. *Naturally the distance a player stands from the ball will vary according to height and build. Standing too near or too far from the ball are both detrimental to the swing. The only way to find your correct distance is to stand upright holding the club horizontally out in front of yourself. Then lower the club to the ground — by bending your back only. This will give you the right distance, and a posture as if you were about to lower yourself on to a tall stool.*

As the right hand is holding the club lower down the shaft than the left, the right shoulder is naturally below the left when the stance is taken up. (See Fig. 18.)

The head is behind the ball and the whole position should seem comfortable and relaxed.

Where the feet are concerned, there are three variations. These are : the square stance with both feet along a line parallel to the intended flight of the ball ; an open stance with right foot slightly forward and left foot taken back ; and a shut (or closed) stance, with left foot slightly forward and right foot back from the line of flight.

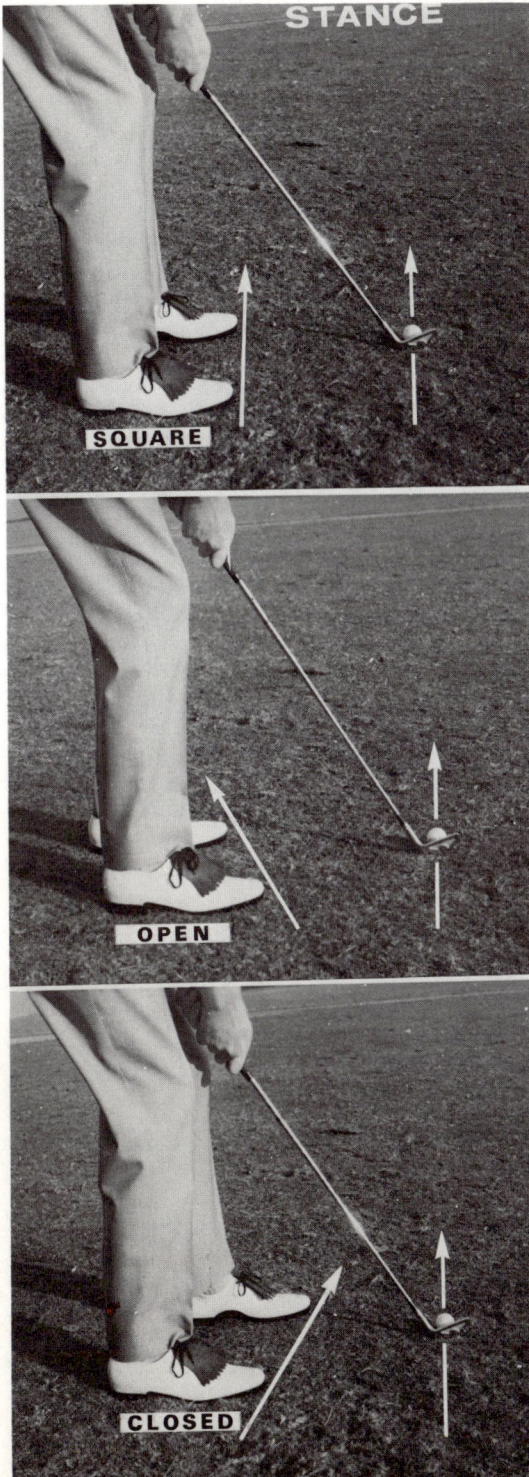

STANCE

SQUARE

OPEN

CLOSED

15. *The three variations of stance.* Square Stance : *both feet parallel to the line of flight.* Open Stance : *left foot an inch or so back from the right foot.* Closed Stance : *left foot in advance of the right foot. The slightly open stance is the one favoured for most shots.*

You will not be wrong to start with the square stance, although experience as a teacher has convinced me that a slightly open stance is best for most players. But only the feet are in a slightly open position. The shoulders stay square for short and mid-iron shots, while for longer shots and the woods the shoulders are slightly closed and pointing just a bit right of target.

During a golf swing on the wind up (backswing) the hips turn around 45 degrees, while the shoulders make a 90 degrees turn. The stance as outlined enables the newcomer to swing freely through the ball.

One of the biggest difficulties is that of lining up accurately for direction. So many pupils think they are aiming at target. For guidance ask somebody to stand behind your clubhead and tell you exactly where you are aiming.

You do not line up through your feet but on a line through the ball. A good way to test your own line of aim is to take up your stance leaning forward over the ball and with knees bent. Then place a club across the front of the shoulders. Where the club is pointing is where you are aiming.

The way I line up is by placing the clubhead squarely behind the ball and imaging a letter 'T' with the tail pointing at the target.

5 IRON   DRIVER

16. (above) *Experience has taught me that for the majority a slightly open stance (right foot slightly in advance of left with the shoulders square or a little closed to the intended line of flight) is best. This may vary slightly from player to player according to physique. A good way to find if you are aiming correctly is to take your stance to the ball and while you are still in position place the club across the shoulders. Where the shaft is pointing is where you are aiming.*

17. *If the backswing is carried out correctly, by the time it is completed the shoulders will have turned through 90 degrees and the hips through 45 degrees. This gives a spring-like wind-up between the two of 45 degrees. For the irons, as seen on the right, the hips turn about 35 degrees owing to the shorter backswing.*

CHAPTER FIVE

Swing

Let's start by making a full swing without a ball.

The swing is one continuous movement from start to finish. It is *not* a series of separate movements joined together. Remember that, it is important.

My basic teaching has always been that all body movements respond automatically to the direction in which the clubhead is made to travel, controlled by the hands in a swinging action; it is *not* the other way round.

Before going further I feel it is apt here that I quote two sayings by that great teaching professional, the late Ernest Jones, who said: 'You don't make movement to move the clubhead. You move the clubhead to make movement.' Obviously moving the clubhead by a swinging action.

Jones also said:

'A centipede was happy quite, until a toad in fun said "Pray which leg goes after which?" This put his mind in such a fix, he fell distracted in a ditch, considering how to run.'

However, I *reluctantly* have to break down the swing in order to explain what happens. I much prefer to emphasise that the secret of a good golf swing is to think only of the clubhead and the path

on which it should travel.

But if the swing does have to be broken down, then it involves six parts:

1. Address position.

2. From the address position to waist high on the backswing — and the backswing is the slowest part of the whole swing. At address your arms and the clubshaft form a letter 'Y'.

The clubhead is not taken straight back from the ball but, lightly brushing the turf for as long as possible, it starts to move in a circle. That is, the clubhead is travelling round and up. As it does so the left knee breaks slightly towards the right.

The letter 'Y' must be maintained for as long as possible and the hands and wrists left unbroken.

Don't rush your backswing. You cannot hit anything going back, and the first few feet of your backswing help to determine the success of your shot.

3. Moving from the waist high position to the top of the backswing. At this point you allow the hands to become active and the wrists to break.

The arms continue to swing round and up, but the head stays still. The left shoulder is now under the chin.

At the top of the backswing the left arm

Golf

will be practically straight and the right arm will be bent and under the clubshaft. The hands are as high as the top of the head, and the clubshaft is pointing along the intended line of flight.

Your body has wound up like a spring and the shoulders have turned twice as far as the hips. Most of the weight is on your right foot, in the form of pressing down.

4. Returning to the ball. On the way down, the wrists straighten so that by impact that letter 'Y' has been formed again. In theory you are back at the address position.

5. From striking the ball to waist high. This is just the same as for the start of the backswing, only in reverse. Maintain that letter 'Y' and you

18. *Breaking the swing down into six parts, ignoring the ball position to feet as the illustrations apply to both woods and irons.* Part 1 : *address.* Part 2 : *with clubhead in mind, swing it round and wide to waist high, maintaining the letter 'Y' as formed at address.* Part 3 : *from waist high continue on the same path with your arms moving up and at the same time your wrists breaking until the top of the backswing is reached.* Part 4 : *from the top of the backswing return the clubhead to the ball. In theory only*

will find your right shoulder turning under your chin. The left leg straightens and the right knee moves towards the left leg.

6. The finish of the follow-through. This completes the swing and if the whole movement has been correct it will happen anyway. The wrists bend as the club is thrown up and over your left shoulder.

Now your left arm bends just as your right arm did at the top of the backswing, and the weight has moved on to your left foot. Your body is facing the target and you finish up on your right toe.

I suggest that you spend about 15 minutes just trying the first and second parts. Then on the next day combine parts one, two and three. Add part four on the third day, five and six on the fourth, and then put together the entire swing.

you are now back at the address position. Part 5 : from theoretical impact position swing the clubhead through to waist high. The letter 'Y' should now have returned (the reverse of Part 2). The back of the right hand clubhead should be facing away from you. Part 6 : from waist high on the follow-through throw the clubhead up and over your left shoulder. This will hinge your wrists correctly. Spend some time practising these movements — 1 with 2, then 1, 2 and 3, and so on until the movements become joined.

Golf

However, I am much more concerned with flowing rather than frozen movement.

How fast you swing (and the swing involves a gradual build up of speed starting from the slow backswing), can vary from player to player. If a certain speed seems right for you, then stick with it.

19. This is Sam Snead. Now refer back to Part 4 of Fig. 18. At impact, theoretically, Sam is back at his address position but due to the movement through the swing his left hip has turned out of the way, the right shoulder has gone down a little, with the left shoulder going up in response. It shows there is little difference between theory and movement through the swing as far as the 6-part illustration is concerned.

Nor is there any such thing as one copybook swing. The swings of champions like Tony Jacklin, Arnold Palmer, Jack Nicklaus, Ben Hogan, Lee Trevino, Johnny Miller, Hale Irwin and many others, are all as different as their fingerprints. What they have in common is that they swing the clubhead and at impact return the clubface squarely to the back of the ball.

A swing should be as smooth and rhythmic as the pendulum of a clock moving backwards and forwards. The player who is swinging smoothly seems to use little effort. *It should be effortless power, not powerful effort.* Now that you understand the six parts of a swing you can concentrate instead on producing one complete rhythmic swing.

20–26. *Learn the basics first if you want to progress like these star players. Owing to differing physiques and mental make-up they all have their individual swings, as different as their fingerprints. Do not copy a champion of the day because a swing shape suiting one player does not necessarily suit another. The picture of Jack Nicklaus shows the general swing track of top-class players. The lines are not drawn but captured by my camera with Jack using my patented 'X-Ray' equipment.*

20. Tony Jacklin.

21. Arnold Palmer.

22. Jack Nicklaus.

23. Ben Hogan.

24. Lee Trevino.

25. Johnny Miller.

26. Hale Irwin.

Only one thing is going to make contact with the ball and that is the clubhead. *That clubhead is what you should have in your mind*. Don't think of making specific body movements. They will happen automatically if you are swinging correctly.

We don't want a chain of individual movements, we want a swing. A swing with a strike incorporated. And you are not hitting at a ball. You should concentrate on swinging through – taking the attitude that the ball is a mere obstacle in the way of your clubhead as it swings through.

SWINGING POWER NOT POWERFUL EFFORT

27. *When watching professionals, never copy swing movements but try to capture the rhythm of their swing. A clock pendulum with its constant smooth swing is the best mental picture for the golfer to follow in order to gain the best results. It is only natural that if this form is in mind when swinging the clubhead a strike will take place within the swing – giving both power and accuracy to the shot.*

CHAPTER SIX

The Irons

Having dealt with grip, stance and the basics of a golf swing, we move on to the irons. I suggest you start with the short irons since they are easier to control. That means the 8- and 9-irons. These are clubs for attacking the flagstick, but resist any temptation to strain for distance.

The short clubs are precision irons, and a three-quarter length swing with them is the equivalent of a full-swing. Don't try swinging them round your neck. Accuracy not distance is the object. Here's a rule to tuck away : the shorter the club, the shorter the swing and the narrower the stance.

Feel in your mind that you swing all clubs — woods and irons — the same way. But because the 8- and 9-irons have short shafts it means you will be standing closer to the ball, and through this you will automatically get a more upright swing.

The difference is built into the club. In general terms you use an 8-iron when popping at the green from 100 to 120 yards, 9-iron for 80 to 100 yards or wedge for 60 to 80 yards.

The stance ? Feet slightly open (left toe a fraction back from the right), shoulders square, and the *back* of the ball

28. My son Kelvin, 19 years old and handicap 1, swinging a 9-iron to three-quarter backswing. It is equivalent to a full swing with a longer club. Accuracy and not distance is the object.

As the ball is centred for the 8- and 9-iron shot it means it will be struck before the clubhead has reached the bottom of its arc.

You hit the ball down and through, and take a divot (a small piece of turf) after the ball has been struck. Taking divots is a commendable feature of good iron play. And remember good golfers always replace divots !

This shot involves minimal body action. The knees are flexed, the wrists cock on their own early in the backswing, and the hands are a trifle ahead of the club blade at impact.

29. *Johnny Miller playing a short iron, the ball positioned opposite the centre of his feet. Note that even the golfing greats have to practise.*

positioned level with the centre line between the feet. The reason for this ball position is that the club strikes a descending blow which produces maximum backspin. The ball is intended to land on the green and as it does so the backspin helps it to check and may possibly bring it back a few feet.

If you take up your stance with the ball towards your front foot, i.e. left of centre, then the ball will fly higher. The more the ball moves back in the stance, the greater the likelihood of a lower-flying shot. (See Fig. 55.)

30. *These pictures show the difference between a wedge at impact and a longer iron. With the longer iron the clubhead passes the hands at impact and just after, but when playing the wedge the hands are kept in front throughout the action.*

Golf

Avoid the usual trap beginners fall into of wanting to see the ball fly high and trying to help it by scooping. The club blade can do it without any help.

A short and crisp shot is better than a long and easy one, and if you are using these clubs off a tee make sure that you tee the ball up very close to the grass.

31. As with the 8- and 9-irons and wedge the hands are a fraction in front of the clubhead at impact. This will happen if you trust the loft of the club to elevate the ball for you. The error when playing this shot is that the player attempts to help the loft to get the ball into the air. This usually happens when playing over greenside obstacles, and a scooping action occurs. You may hit a fair shot but more likely a fluff or a topped shot will result.

Both these clubs are ones you will need to know and master in order to play good golf and score well. You should feel confident of hitting the green every time you use them. You can take them in the rough as well as off the fairway and ideally, with practice and experience, you will be aiming to leave the ball close enough to the hole to get down in one putt. (See Fig. 58.)

The mid-irons are the 5-, 6- and 7-irons and these again ought not to present much of a headache. The 5-iron is a good club for general swing practice, and most beginners tell me it is their favourite club. Your 5-, 6- and 7-irons should be knocking the ball from 110 up to 125 yards. (See Fig. 3.)

Being longer than the 8- and 9-irons, the mid-irons will automatically make you stand further away from the ball. Position the ball just left of centre, between the feet for the 7-iron, and move it an inch or so towards the left foot for the 5- and 6-irons.

Always practise with a *specific target in view* and you will realise as you start to use the longer clubs that the longer the shot, the more important it is to aim accurately. *Take a line through the ball* and *not* through your toes.

Although the stance is slightly wider, the feet are still in an open position, the hands are opposite the ball at address and the shoulders are square to the intended line of flight.

The ball is struck first, and the turf afterwards. It is a sort of squeezing effect between clubface and turf, with the club going on through the ball.

A problem we now face as the swing becomes longer is that of bringing the right shoulder into the shot. It has to be kept out. So feel that the clubhead arrives first at the ball and that the shoulders are square to the ball at impact. (See Figs. 41 and 42.)

When it comes to the long irons, the Nos. 3 and 4, avoid the illusion of thinking that because the ball has to go further you have to hit consciously harder. Only hit as hard as your hands and arms allow. It helps if you feel you are still playing a 9-iron and use the same pace. The extra distance will be obtained because it is a longer club involving a longer swing.

I recommend a three-quarter swing. The reason is that accuracy is still important although it is a longer shot, and a less-than-full shot helps with control. Try to feel that a three-quarter shot is a full shot and then you will be playing within yourself.

If you are in any doubt about whether the lie of the ball is good enough, then forget the 3-iron. Never use it in the rough, but if the ball is sitting up nicely in semi-rough then you could get away with it.

The 4-iron is more of a favourite with most amateurs and can despatch a ball 180 to 190 yards when used in the right way. I suggest you get to know it before tackling the 3-iron.

The ball is positioned about one-third of the way between your left foot and the centre of your stance. Your weight is more on the right foot than the left in a 60–40 proportion, and the right shoulder is well below the left.

The stance should be slightly open with the left shoulder aiming a little right of target. Beware of tension creeping into the shot, and reduce it by flexing the knees.

LOW BACK

32. A three-quarter swing using a 3-iron is longer in comparison to a three-quarter swing with a 9-iron. Check with Fig. 28. Note how the club is parallel to the intended line of flight – as it should be.

33. At the start of the backswing keep the clubhead low by brushing the turf lightly for about 15 inches as it swings round on an inclined plane to the top of

Swing the clubhead back close to the ground and remember to make the hands and arms do the work.

You may find that you slice the ball and this is caused by the clubhead arriving at

the ball too late. The hands are in front at this point.

I can give you a correction. Indeed, it is an over-correction. *Practise by feeling that the clubhead is going to reach the*

LOW THRU

HANDS
AHEAD

CLUBHEAD
LATE

the backswing. Through the impact area also keep it low to the ground, resulting in extension through the swing.

ball before the hands. It may seem to do so, but what really happens is that clubhead and hands arrive together.

34. Assuming you have swung correctly but the ball curves to the right you can be sure that your hands were in front at impact. This automatically keeps the clubface open. This fault can be cured by an over-correction — that is, feel the clubhead will arrive back at the ball first.

CHAPTER SEVEN

Practice – Learning to Strike

Now you should go out to the practice ground. That is the only way to improve. Through practice certain movements get ingrained as habit, and as a result we obtain what is called 'muscle memory'.

Start by taking a full swing *without* a ball being involved. Make sure you stick to the basics just described because too often pupils revert to their natural swing.

And check your grip as that has a habit of going awry.

Now we are going to introduce a ball to get the feel of hitting one. I want you to start with a half-swing, that is from waist high on the backswing to waist high on the follow-through. Over a period of time you can introduce a little wrist movement, but still sticking with the half-swing.

When that has been mastered you can go on to increase the length of swing until a full swing for the club in question has been achieved. An ideal to-and-fro swing pace is the tempo of the tune Blue Danube.

When you start practising with a ball put it down on a good lie and, assuming you are using a 5-, 6- or 7-iron, take up your stance with the ball positioned just left of centre.

There is a rule about the positioning of feet to ball at the address. The longer the club the more the ball is positioned towards the front foot. The shorter the club, the more the ball moves back towards the middle of the stance. (See Fig. 13.)

Don't hit *at* the ball but swing through, and no matter what the result of the shots, stick to your taught swing rather than your old one.

You must not expect results to come all at once. Give them time and they will.

After a while you will find that the ball is travelling a degree or more off line. This is caused by the clubface being open or closed in the striking zone, or your swing track may be out of line.

What you are seeking, and you cannot expect to race ahead immediately, is a mysterious thing called 'feel'. Another way of putting it is that the hands must become 'educated'.

The best way to learn how an open or closed clubface (open means the heel of the club is closer to the ball than the toe, while closed means the toe of the club is closer) is to experiment on the putting green. Hit a few putts with an open face and then with a closed face. Then you will appreciate how the hands control the clubface through a swing.

35. First get the feel of hitting a ball on the putting green, then try a few chip shots (short shots) up to 40 yards, using a 7- or 8-iron. When it comes to playing longer shots with the same club, swing to waist high on the backswing through to about waist high on the follow-through. When this has been mastered, introduce a little wrist action on the backswing by breaking the wrists (hinge effect). Like everything else in life, we have to learn to walk before we can run.

Golf

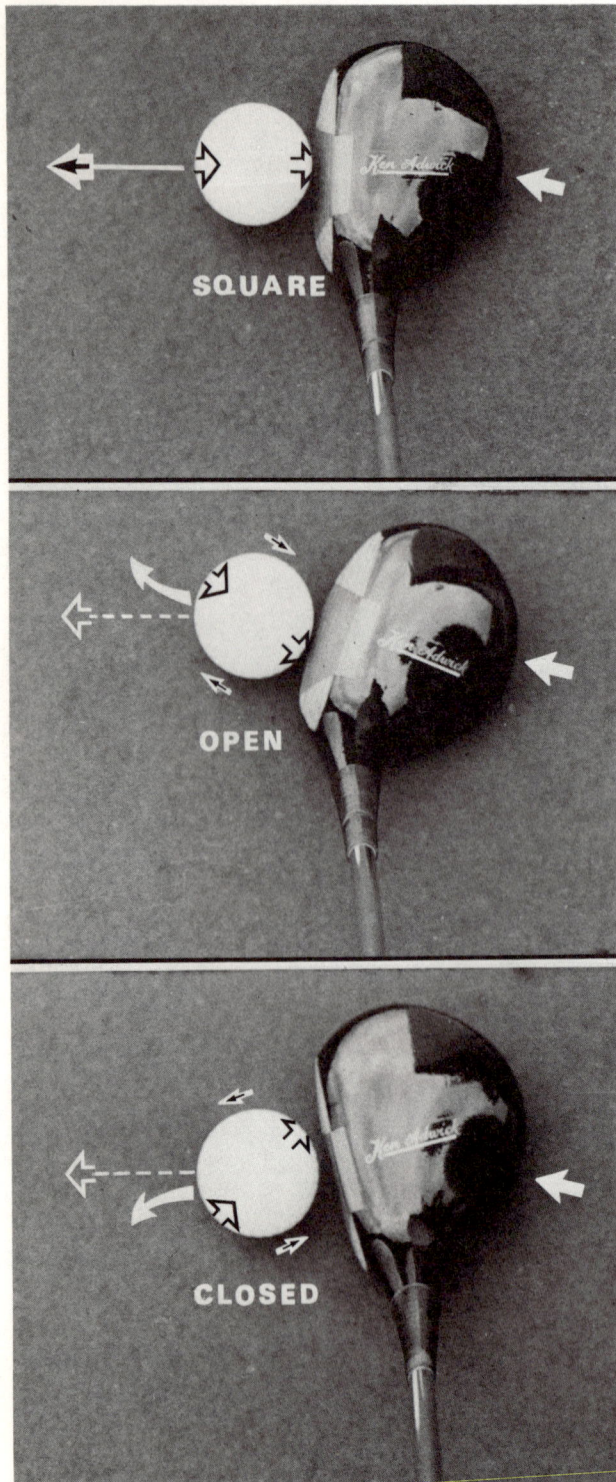

36. The position of the clubface when square, open or closed. The arrows indicate the direction the ball will fly when the club meets the ball at the different angles, assuming that the swing path through the ball is correct – that is, from inside-to-straight.

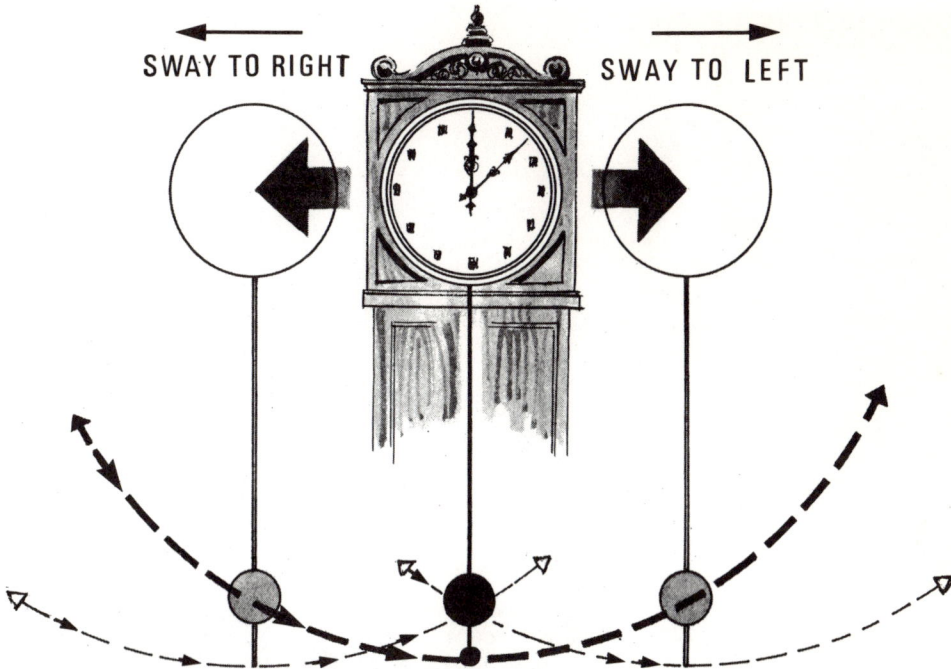

SWAY TO RIGHT   SWAY TO LEFT

37. One of the hardest things to do when learning is to swing freely and at the same time keep your head still. A sway in either direction will most certainly move the bottom of your swing arc in the applicable direction. The ball is still and your head should also remain still throughout the swing, while the body will rotate – known as the pivot. A good tip is to imagine your body as a grandfather clock, the arms and clubshaft acting as its pendulum. It will now be easy to see how the bottom of the swing arc is thrown out of position should a sway to the left or right take place.

Another time, try the same experiment with an 8-iron. Hit open shots, closed ones and then some with the clubface square. Knowing for certain the clubface is square at impact during a swing is that elusive factor called 'feel'.

While you are learning to swing do not forget that the body must remain still. A sway backwards or forwards will move the bottom of your swing arc in the same direction. Naturally your body will turn a little.

If you like, imagine that your lower body is inside a barrel, and that as you turn your sides must not come in contact with the sides of that barrel.

Again, you can imagine that your head is the centre of a wheel and the rim of the wheel is running around you on an inclined plane. If the rim is grooved the clubhead follows that groove right through the swing.

So you now have the rudiments of a good golf swing and should be appreciating at this stage how vital the hands are in the game. *Remember the hands are the tools of the brain.*

Golf

38. *As you swing the clubhead, feel it is running round the rim of an imaginary wheel placed around you, with your head as the hub and the wheel positioned at an angle a little to the right of target. This gives you a track on the backswing inside to the intended line of flight.*

39. (facing page) *The amateur on the right has swayed into the shot, which results in an incorrect finish. His body instead of his hands and arms has swung the club, and every bad shot in the game can result from this. Neil Coles, on the left, displays a copy book finish by swinging the clubhead back and through. In response to this action the body merely rotates and does not move out of the space it occupied at the time of address. 'X' marks the spot from where the the ball was played.*

46

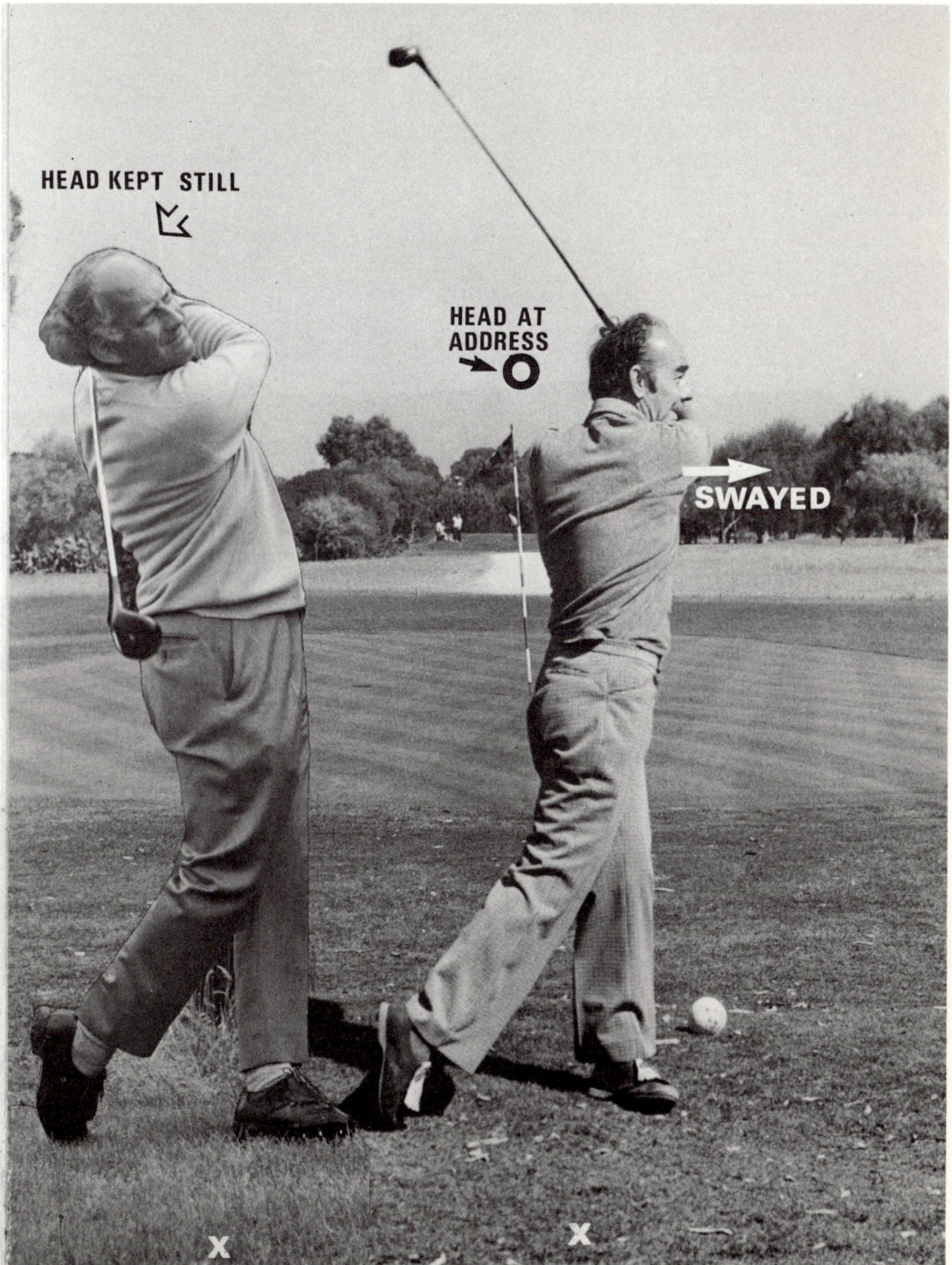

HEAD KEPT STILL

HEAD AT ADDRESS

SWAYED

Golf

What you have to do is to develop 'feel', and the answer to that is *the most beneficial exercise in golf*. It is simply to stand with feet together and touching, and swing a 6- or 7-iron. Whether or not a ball is used is immaterial at first.

Obviously we stand with feet apart when we want to stabilise balance. By placing the feet together we are bound to lose balance if we use body muscles in the shot instead of hand and arm action. I kept my eldest son, now a professional, at this exercise for three months. It is swing power we are developing and not

SWING BACK AND THROUGH

40. *The only exercise in golf to produce that indefinable 'feel' (which has to be learned and cannot be taught) is to swing the clubhead with your feet together and touching. Good balance is the result of good swinging. For every effect there has to be a cause, and not the other way round.*

muscle power. The muscle power we produce has to be converted into clubhead speed. Then you have a smooth and rhythmical swing and good timing.

Please stick with the feet-together exercise. It keeps the right shoulder out of the shot, develops a good hand action, aids balance, makes the body stay still, builds up left side control and, best of all,

gives the feel of a swinging motion.

One of the snags with golf is that so many players think they have to introduce the big body muscles into the shot when they are striving for distance. What they are doing is heaving or levering. It does not work that way at all. The hands can do the job if you will let them. It is the rank amateur who recognises force by heaving movements.

41. Well-known comedian Ronnie Corbett, a keen golfer, has heaved his body into this shot in an endeavour to hit the ball a long way. He has exchanged swing power for muscle power. This has made his right shoulder turn into the shot with the ball being despatched well to the left of the direction in which he was aiming, the clubhead travelling from out-to-in.

42. In contrast to Ronnie Corbett, Arnold Palmer has swung the clubhead from inside-to-straight which has made his right shoulder go down and under, and his elbow is nearer to his body than that of Ronnie Corbett. Compare also the right foot of both players. These different body actions are a direct result of the clubhead being swung on different swing paths. The body follows the clubhead, not the other way round.

Golf

That feet-together exercise will prove for you how important a part the hands play and you will be surprised how far you can hit a ball when just using hands and arms. No time spent on this exercise is ever wasted — and I tell my pupils to go on practising it until they are sick of doing so, and then still keep on.

You can do this exercise with one hand on the club and the other hand behind the back. After a while use the other hand on its own.

But make sure you do more swinging with the left hand because most golfers experience trouble due to their right side — the stronger side — wanting to dominate the shot. It is what we call right-side domination.

Yet it is the left side that has to control the swing. So we have to strengthen the left hand, arm and side, and slacken off on the natural right side. The opposite applies for the left-handed player.

WRIST

43. Feet together and touching, using one hand with the other behind your back. This is a good exercise to help with control, feel, balance and to strengthen the hands. Here I am using my right hand only. Better to hit more shots with the left hand only than with the right, say 80 shots with the left to 20 with the right hand.

44. A most important exercise is to swing the club with left hand only, feet together and touching. It is essential after striking the ball to allow the clubhead only to go on, leaving your left arm almost opposite your left side. This will strengthen your left hand and forearm. It is a waist high to waist high action.

CHAPTER EIGHT

The Woods

Now we get to the power clubs, the woods, that so many of you novices are impatient to use. Including, of course, the most powerful club of all, the big boomer — the driver.

There is a 5-wood which gets the ball into the air quickly and seems to suit most women players. But the 4-wood is really the first of the wooden clubs to consider.

It is easy to use, has a good degree of loft and is understandably popular. Nearly all players carry a 4-wood and it has so many uses that it is always kept busy. Tee, fairway or semi-rough, you can use the 4-wood almost anywhere.

But it has its limitations. It is not as accurate as a 3-iron, it is hard to make a wood shot stop on the green, and it can present problems when used into wind. Under normal conditions you could clock up around 200 yards, more likely 180 yards.

The beginner often likes to drive with a No. 3 wood, although its real purpose is as a power fairway club. It also comes into the reckoning at the long par-three holes.

You need a fairly good lie to hit a 3-wood with certainty and when doubt creeps in then the 4-wood will do a better job.

45. The 4-wood is popular with lady golfers. Here it is used by Sandra Haynie, an American professional tournament player. As a style study, note how her left hip has turned out of the way in response to the clubhead swinging through, without her right shoulder having entered the shot.

Hit correctly, you might get as much as between 190–220 yards from a 3-wood.

The 2-wood is also meant to be a fairway club, but a whole army of golfers use it off the tee because they find it safer and more reliable than a driver.

If, as a beginner, you are only going to carry half the woods, then I must point out that you should opt for a 2-wood and a 4-wood rather than a 1-wood and a 3-wood.

Never use the 2-wood off the fairway unless the lie is excellent, and you should also refrain from trying to force those extra few yards from it. The reason why handicap golfers like the 2-wood is that the extra loft gives them confidence and there is a greater margin for error. Even players able to use a driver will choose to drop to a 2-wood when faced with a narrow fairway from the tee. It is a good club against the wind from the fairway and with the wind behind is used for driving off the tee, to send the ball sail-like up into the helping wind.

The ball is placed in the same position for these woods, whether the shot is from tee or fairway. It is some two inches inside the left heel.

The stance is slightly open with shoulder line pointing just right of target. The feet are wider apart than for iron shots, and the swing is a little slower and longer.

Flex your knees, make sure your left arm and clubshaft are practically in a straight line, but don't crouch. (See Fig. 13.)

Try for a wide swing arc and it will help to maintain that arc if the wrists do not break until later in the backswing.

Again, the danger is the old mental block of thinking the ball has to travel a long way, which means 'I shall have to hit it harder, and never mind the hands, I'll heave away with my body muscles'. (See Fig. 41.) That way the shot is ruined before you make it. *Swing power through the hands is the answer*.

The driver should be the easiest club in the bag to use. The ball is on a tee, the ground is flat, and the clubhead is large. The reason so many players find it difficult is the problem already mentioned of thinking it is necessary to hit harder and exert more power when using a powerful club.

You have to relax just as much with a driver as with any other club, otherwise your muscles tighten up and hand action is reduced. There is another factor to remember — that any error is magnified by the distance the ball is about to travel. Lack of loft can also magnify error.

So much of the difficulty is in the mind. The first thing to do when using a driver is tee the ball up with half of it showing above the clubface. It should be positioned just inside the left heel, the purpose of this being that by the time the club reaches the ball it will have passed the lowest point of the swing arc and will be striking the ball on the start of the upswing. (See Fig. 13.)

As before, the stance is feet slightly open and shoulders fractionally closed pointing right of target or closed to the feet line. That shoulder position will help your backswing to start off on an inside path. But if you find a stance with feet and shoulders square suits you better, then by all means try it.

To help with relaxation take a practice swing, flex the knees, and waggle the club in a kind of miniature swing-to-come. Avoid a vice-like grip.

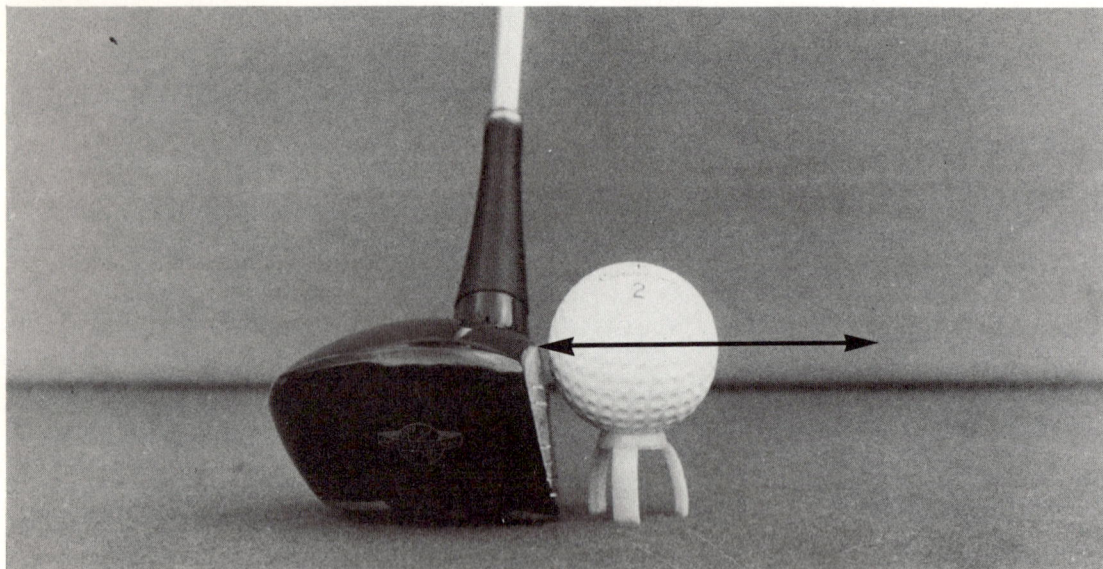

46. *When using the driver it is favourable to have the ball elevated with half the ball showing above the clubface. From this position the ball can be swept off the tee-peg. The ball is positioned opposite a spot just inside the left heel and if the club is swung correctly the ball will be struck at the start of the upswing.*

47. (facing page) *Should the club be picked up from the ball the wrists break too soon with no shoulder turn. The backswing then becomes steep and narrow in response. A whole chain of disastrous reactions takes place, resulting in bad shots. The correct way to start the backswing is to keep the clubface looking at the ball as it sweeps back close to the ground, round and on an inclined plane. Done correctly, the letter 'Y' formed by arms and clubshaft will be intact to almost waist high. The shoulders will turn and a wide and proper backswing will result. A good start to the backswing is essential to good swinging.*

The feet are as wide apart as the shoulders – that is for most people, depending on physique – with the hands level with the front side of the ball. Feel that the left side of your face is behind the ball and have your right elbow flexed towards your body.

All of this may sound complicated but comes easily and instinctively after a short while.

The club is swung back – *not picked up*. Repeat, do *not* pick up the club. Otherwise it is the same swing as with your other clubs. But, of course, you will be standing a little further from the ball owing to the length of the clubshaft. So the swing becomes naturally flatter.

Maintain that 'Y' formed by arms (*without rigidity*) *and clubshaft for as long as possible because a wide backswing is going to help with power. Take your time on the backswing – nobody else is going to move the ball – and then with speed increasing as you return to the ball sweep it off the tee.*

OPEN

WRONG

CORRECT

SQUARE

Golf

As you return to the ball a whiplash action takes place from the top of the backswing. As an over-correction it helps nature if you concentrate on getting the clubhead to the ball before the hands.

That automatically frees the hands and allows the clubhead to be released in the striking area. The club is free-wheeling and clubhead speed is increased. (See Fig. 19.)

The feeling should be that *your head stays still* throughout the action, and take care not to dip the left shoulder at the top of the backswing. The left shoulder moves round and under the chin, not downwards.

Try to limit the length of swing and keep the clubface looking at the ball for as long as possible as it moves back from the ball.

Stay down on the ball and do not be too anxious to lift your head and see where the shot has gone. You should finish with the hands high, shoulders and trouser-belt buckle facing target, and balanced on your left foot and right toe.

48. (left) *Whiplash. The downswing has started . . . the transition from backswing to downswing plus the weight of the clubhead has cocked the wrists automatically to maximum, and so the clubhead will momentarily still be going back as the downswing starts. Two body reactions are quite noticeable: my left foot is pressing down in opposition and my right leg is sloping more in reponse. These and other movements occur naturally through the swinging movement of the clubhead. This chain reaction will not take place if the grip on the club is too rigid at the start of the swing. To the onlooker, it may seem that I am pulling down with the left hand and arm; in fact I am doing the opposite in trying to return the clubhead to the ball first, in order to neutralise this natural 'flail-like' action. If this is not done the hands would be in front of the clubhead at impact – late hitting.*

49. *Tournament star Johnny Miller in practice for the Open Championship. He has swung well through the ball, finishing well balanced on his left foot and right toe. (He would only have to turn his left foot towards target to put himself in a walking position.) His hands are high, head still over the spot where the ball was at the start of the swing. These points are a chain reaction to a good backswing, coupled with a swinging action.*

CHAPTER NINE

Bunkers

No matter how good a golfer is, there will be times when he is faced with the prospect of playing a ball out of a bunker. These come in all sizes, and the first consideration is to get out.

The trouble is that so many players are seized by fright when they see sand. Yet the operation is relatively simple. You could call it the easiest shot of all because it has a great margin for error.

To get out of a bunker we use a sand iron. It has a rounded sole to stop the blade digging too deep into the sand, and is the heaviest club in the bag.

Whether the sand is hard or soft you should resist the temptation to try to chip out. The best way is the explosion shot — that is, taking plenty of sand with the shot.

We want to make the ball rise quickly, so the stance we adopt is with the feet in an exaggerated open position with the ball positioned opposite the left *heel*.

A word of warning : inside a bunker the clubhead must not touch a grain of sand while addressing the ball or during the backswing, otherwise a penalty is incurred.

The hands are just ahead of the ball and while the clubface is kept square to the line of flight the club is swung parallel to the line of the feet.

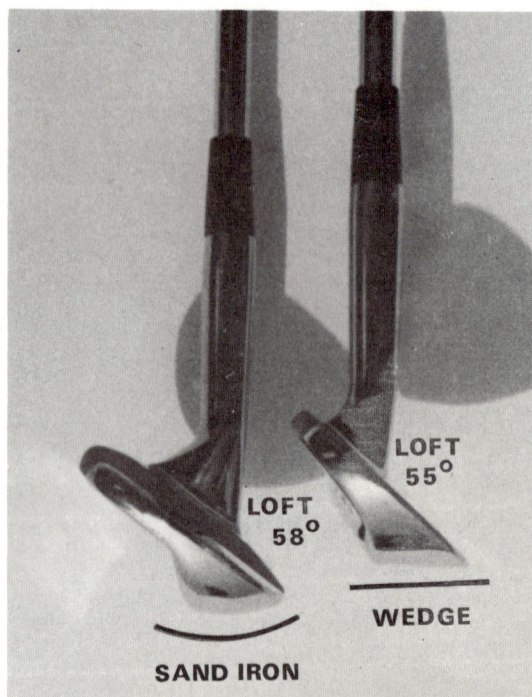

50. Sand Iron : *the heaviest club in the bag and designed for bunker play. The front edge is raised to help stop it digging into the sand, and the back edge is lower. The whole sole is curved. Wedge : designed to produce maximum backspin for short approach and delicate shots around the green. With this club the front is lower than the back edge, and the sole flat as against the sand iron. Practice is worthwhile with this club; used correctly it can be your best friend; used incorrectly it will be your worst enemy.*

OPEN STANCE

SWING PATH

C/FACE OPEN

51. *Bunker Shot. Escaping from bunkers is simple if you adopt an open stance (left foot 3 to 4 inches back from right) with the ball positioned opposite the left heel, bottom edge of clubface in line with target. Then swing the club slowly and deliberately parallel to your feet line (an out-to-in swing), taking sand before the ball, and go on to a full follow-through, keeping your hands in front throughout the action. The rules state that the clubhead must not touch sand prior to the swing.*

Golf

The result is an out-to-in swing with a steepish backswing. Then you sweep down, under and through, striking sand about one inch before the ball. It has been said that the bunker shot is the only one where you do not actually touch the ball. The clubhead takes sand and moves the ball out as it passes underneath. Be sure to *continue to a full follow-through* and do not leave the clubhead buried in the sand. The swing itself must be full, slow and deliberate. It is a hand and arm shot with legs and body hardly involved. But before playing it you should move your feet about in the sand, seeking a firm foothold.

Remember to keep the shot going and to hit past yourself. The perfect bunker shot has the ball rising steeply, sand sprayed, and will help with the ball dropping dead or spinning back.

Sometimes a ball ends in a fairway bunker a considerable distance from the green. Here we not only want to escape but to get some distance, too.

From nearby turf, for example, you may use a 2- or 3-iron for the distance required, or even a wood. Never be tempted to use such clubs to get out of any bunker, no matter how shallow – it is not worth the risk.

I would say a 4-iron is the 'largest' club worth considering. Other factors influence the final choice. Should the ball be sitting nicely, then you have to decide what club will get it up quickly enough to clear the bunker bank or lip. It is no good taking a powerful club and smacking the ball into the bunker face.

If the ball is partly buried, then you must settle for an explosion shot. After all, I opened with the comment that the most important thing was to get back on

52. *Gary Player, the finest bunker player in the world. This picture confirms the caption to Fig. 51 and is worth careful study.*

turf and into play.

To play a long shot from a fairway bunker, using, say, a 5- or 6-iron, the ball is midway between the feet or even right of centre, with clubface square and hands just ahead. You *must* hit the ball first and take it cleanly. Unlike the explosion shot you do not take sand first.

Don't forget, though, that your prime consideration must not be distance to be covered but which club has enough loft

53. *Fairway Bunker. When distance is required, stand with the ball in a central position or just right of centre if a lower trajectory is required, depending, of course, on how the ball is sitting and on the height of the bunker face to be cleared. With this type of shot the ball, not the sand, must be struck first. Again, the clubhead must not be grounded at address.*

to clear the bunkerside or face.

What about the drill when a bunker is wet or there is no sand in it? Play the shot as if it were off turf.

Don't be ashamed when bunkered with a really bad lie to play out backwards or sideways if necessary, and if you fall foul of one of those colossal bunkers rising like a house wall, then play the ball off your left toe, open the clubface to excess, cut across the ball from out-to-in, and use your strength in this instance.

CHAPTER TEN

The Wedge Shots

Two of the most important shots in the game, the strokesavers that enable you to land close enough to the flagstick to single putt, are the pitch and the chip-and-run.

The wedge is the club used for short approach and delicate pitch shots — pinseekers. It takes time to learn how to master this club but it is time well spent because the player who can use his wedge can snatch a hole or get himself back into a match when all seems lost. When you consider, too, that the wedge is the club used for playing out of thick rough, for lofting shots over trees, bare lies around the green, and awkward shots off paths, then it is obviously going to be a utility club you will use often.

The wedge looks similar to the sand iron but has a straight flat sole which helps it to bite through turf. (See Fig. 50.) The principal shot to be played with the wedge is that lofted shot pitching close to the pin with a degree of backspin. That is to say, after the ball pitches it may even spin back towards the player, if the green is soft enough.

You take a narrow stance with the feet in an open position, which means left foot back from the right. The shoulders are square or a little open to the intended

54. The main purpose of the wedge is for vital approach and pitch shots around the green, also as a utility club for playing out of thick rough, lofting the ball over trees, on bare lies . . . and more. As with any other club, always practise to a target.

line of flight. The wedge and the sand iron are the shortest clubs of all, so you will be standing closer to the ball. The wedge is normally played from the centre of the feet with the hands a little in front of the clubhead. This address position will mean that your backswing is automatically steeper. The shot is played almost without body movement as a hand-and-arm action.

AVERAGE, LOW & HIGH SHOTS

55. *Three address positions for varying shots when using the wedge. For the average shot the ball is positioned in the centre of the stance; for a low shot, opposite the right heel; for a high shot, opposite the left heel. In all three address positions the hands must be in line with the left hip which automatically gives you the position of your hands in relation to the ball.*

Golf

Your wrists will break sooner than on other shots and since you are looking for accuracy rather than distance do not allow the swing to become too long.

The weight is evenly distributed and you must make sure you carry through to a good three-quarter finish. Hit the ball first and take the turf afterwards. The descending blow, with the ball being pinched between clubface and turf, is

56. 11-year-old David Morgan is overswinging with his wedge, so will not achieve accurate results. The club is designed for accuracy and not for distance. Only a three-quarter swing is required. A perfect example is displayed here by Lee Trevino – open and narrow stance, and with the object in mind to pinch the ball between clubface and turf, creating maximum backspin. The name of the club is appropriate as it should be wedged at impact between ball and turf.

what produces the backspin or makes the ball stop dead on the green.

If you practise with this club and learn to use it with confidence, then it will pay many rewards. But avoid falling into the trap of thinking that you have conquered the wedge and that it will play itself.

The cardinal sin is to try to help the club loft the ball. *Any attempt at scooping is fatal*. The loft of the clubface will do it for you. It seems obvious, yet many golfers make the error of scooping. (See Fig. 31.)

If you want to hit a low wedge shot, then the ball is positioned back towards the right foot and the hands are kept in front at impact.

Obviously, for a high shot, the ball is played more off the left foot with the hands in line with the clubhead. They should be near this same position at impact. Make sure you swing right through.

The pitch shot involves delicate precision and a good touch. And don't stand too far from the ball otherwise you will get a flat swing instead of the upright one required.

When your ball is in heavy rough, then use the wedge or a sand iron to escape. You must not be greedy or expect precision, as you are more or less forcing the ball out. You take a steep backswing (to keep the long grass out of the shot as much as possible) and try to swing through the ball. Probably you will have to settle for a stab or 'rap' shot. Make sure you have a firmer left hand grip than is customary because that stops the clubhead turning at impact, due to the long grass.

The chip-and-run shot is played when the ball is close to the green and there are no obstacles on the way to the pin. It is the shot you use when a putt seems possible but there is too much ground to cover. If you did putt, then the

irregularities of the ground would take the ball off line or check it, and the shot would become much too chancy.

57. *When you have strayed into the rough your main aim is to get back into play by using one of the two heaviest clubs in the bag which have the most loft – sand iron or wedge. As these clubs are shorter in length, you will naturally be standing nearer the ball than with the longer clubs. This produces a steeper backswing which is ideal for this shot. Grip a little firmer with your left hand, and try to hit the ball first before becoming entangled in the grass.*

Golf

What you are doing with the chip-and-run is taking an iron that will lift the ball slightly above ground and land it on the green. It will then bounce and run its way up to the flagstick.

Whether you use, say, a 5- or 6-iron, or a 7- or 8-iron depends upon circumstance. When you are close to the green and do not need much loft or carry, then the straighter-faced 5- or 6-iron will do the job. Further away you will need more loft and distance and the 7- or 8-irons are the ones to use.

You play the chip shot with a narrow but open stance. It is a hand and arm movement and the action must be slow with emphasis on the clubhead – using a short swing. You will need practice and experience because what you are trying to judge – and only you can decide – is where you want the ball to land on the green.

OPEN & NARROW STANCE

58. (above left) *When playing a short chip-and-run shot, always adopt a very narrow and open stance, using a much straighter faced club than the wedge. The idea is to keep the ball low so it will land on or just short of the green and trickle up towards the hole – hopefully getting near enough for one putt. Always use this shot when there are no obstacles in the way as it is safer than the wedge. Play it slowly and deliberately and try to 'feel' the strength required. Only practice and experience can give you this. The picture is of my father, a retired professional, aged 82, and an expert at this shot.*

59. (above right) *Should you find difficulty playing the chip-and-run, imagine you are putting with a lofted club. Never scoop at the ball to help it into the air. The loft of the club will do the job for you.*

You will have to discover — I repeat, through practice and experience — how hard to hit. To help get the feel and control of the shot, hold the club a little lower down the grip and put your weight on the left foot, keeping your body perfectly still through the stroke.

Should you find difficulty in playing this shot, whether it be with the 5- or 6-irons, 7- or 8-irons, imagine you are putting with a lofted club.

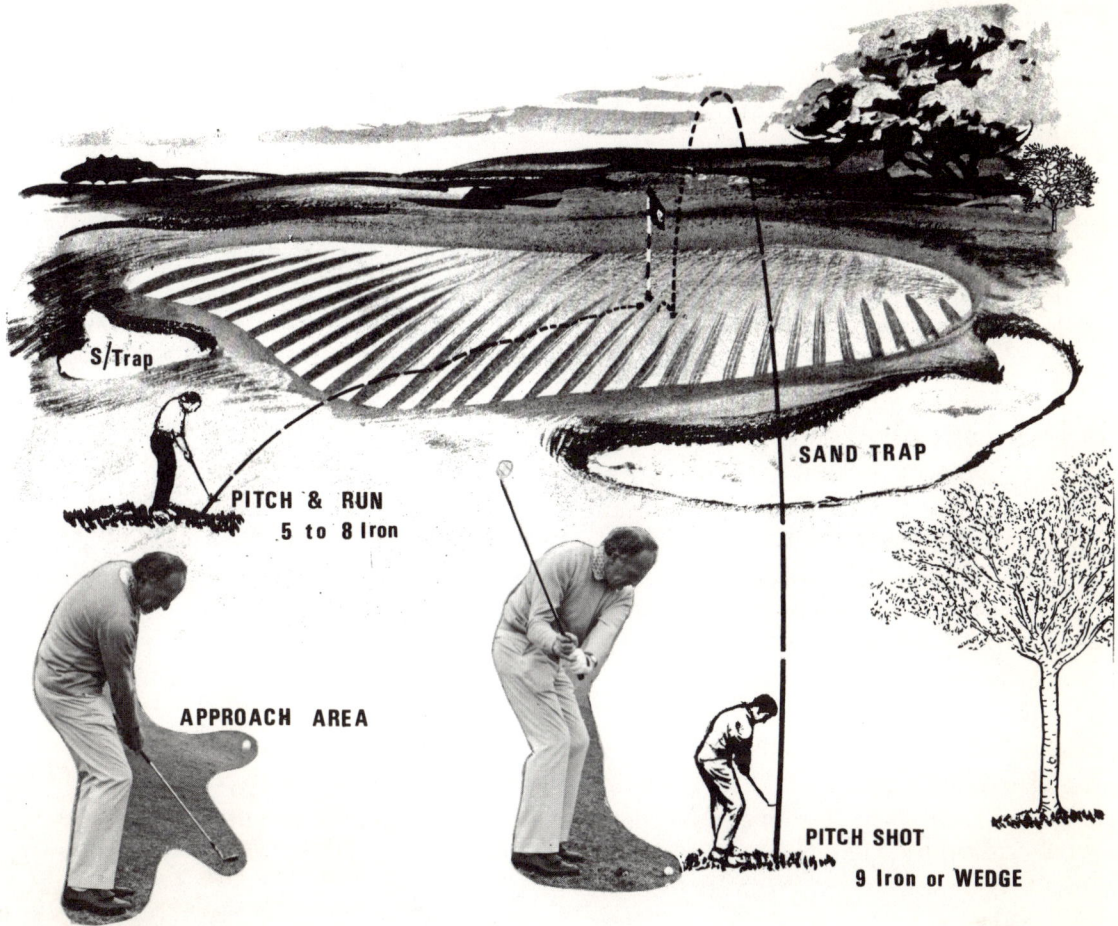

S/Trap

PITCH & RUN
5 to 8 Iron

SAND TRAP

APPROACH AREA

PITCH SHOT
9 Iron or WEDGE

60. The difference between a pitch-and-run and a pitch shot.

CHAPTER ELEVEN

Putting

Putting is something different from the rest of the game and has sometimes been called 'a game within the game'. It is possible to be a poor player from tee to green but a real master with the putter.

The reverse is also true : you can play great golf up to the greens but shaky when it comes to sinking the putts.

Putting frequently accounts for the difference between a high or low score. As I explained earlier, you are allowed in theory two putts for each green, which means that there are 36 putts in a round — or approximately half of your scoring strokes as far as the good player is concerned. So the importance of putting is self-evident.

The top tournament professionals reckon to single putt a share of the greens and take around 28–32 putts for their round.

Most golfers fall into one of three categories when it comes to putting. These are good, inconsistent and poor. The instructor can only help to a certain extent. After that it is up to the individual — and regular practice.

If you can sink 'em with whatever putter you have, then don't bother to change. But in my view a centre-shafted putter is worth a trial.

In general the putter blade should have a little loft, which helps to start the ball straight. And without going too heavy it is better to have a little weight in the head. You can feel it better than a light one.

When putting you *must* keep the body still. The feet are planted sufficiently wide apart to help keep the body still, and the ball is generally positioned inside your left foot ; most have it up to four or five inches inside the toe — as pictured.

61. With putting I have found the best results are obtained when the feet are wide enough apart to stop any fear of swaying, with the ball positioned opposite a point a few inches inside the left foot. Have both feet parallel to the line selected. Gary Player, pictured on the left, adopts a narrow stance with his left toe in advance of his right, and the grip showing that the first finger of his left hand is outside the fingers of his right hand. (Arnold Palmer favours a 'knock-kneed' stance.) But there is no hard and fast rule as to how you putt. The inserted drawing shows A: incorrect arc, too steep. B: correct arc, low back and through.

Golf

You should avoid a position in which your eyes are directly over the ball — and definitely do not have your eyes over the far side of the ball. That invariably results in the ball being putted to the left. It is better to have the eyes slightly your side of the ball, and it will help to discover which is your strongest eye. Do that by

lining up a finger with a distant object. By closing one eye at a time you will find that your master eye is the one that leaves the finger still in line with the object. Now when you putt concentrate on the back of the ball with your best eye. To do that you tilt your head. But don't putt with your weak eye shut.

Otherwise putting is a highly personal thing and if you have a style that suits you, then stick with it.

You will perhaps have seen Arnold Palmer's famous knock-kneed putting stance. He does that to lock the body against movement.

When you are putting have your knees flexed and the weight slightly on your heels and your left side.

As for the grip, if you have your palms opposing it tends to make the elbows spread out. That can lead to faults. What I recommend is to move the two hands fractionally off the front of the shaft and a degree or two round the back. The wrists then hinge correctly and the putter face stays square through the stroke.

It is important to keep the putter blade close to the ground. Low back and low through is the idea.

If you are too wristy then that can introduce inconsistency. It is best to work on a style that gives you a feel for distance.

As for the actual action it is possible to push, tap or stroke a putt. The latter is best.

With a push the putter is held tight and it is easy for the body to move. With tapping it is difficult to judge distance, particularly on long putts. The stroked putt, on the other hand, gives a feel for distance, makes the ball roll straight off the club, and keeps it rolling over the grass without undue bouncing.

The vital factor with distance is how far you take the putter through. One of the best ways to practise for distance is to make a series of lines with strips of cardboard and place them at 3, 5, 7 and 9 yards apart. Then putt a series of balls to each of these lines in turn. (See Fig. 62.) Try to finish on the line or just past, in accordance with the well-known golf saying 'Never up to the hole, never in.'

It also helps to practise putting into a tin smaller than a real golf cup. Then when you finally switch to a proper sized golf cup it will seem that much bigger and easier.

Now you will have to learn to 'read' greens. By that I mean checking for slope, deciding about borrow, knowing whether the green is fast or slow, and what strength is required.

Get down behind the ball when checking on the line. Look at the putt from the side. And once you have made your decision, stick to it.

Curly two-footers worry us all. I think you will hole more than you miss by hitting straight and firm rather than by attempting finesse.

This is something you have to find out for yourself, but bear in mind that a putt is never missed until it has passed the hole.

62. *Generally speaking, better results are obtained if the eyes are looking at a spot an inch or so to your own side of the ball. It helps lining up. If your eyes at address are over a point on the far side of the ball, as deliberately posed by professional Tony Phillips* (left), *then this will be a disadvantage* (even though I have on occasions seen good putters adopt this style). *It is impossible to convey how hard to strike a ball for a given distance.*

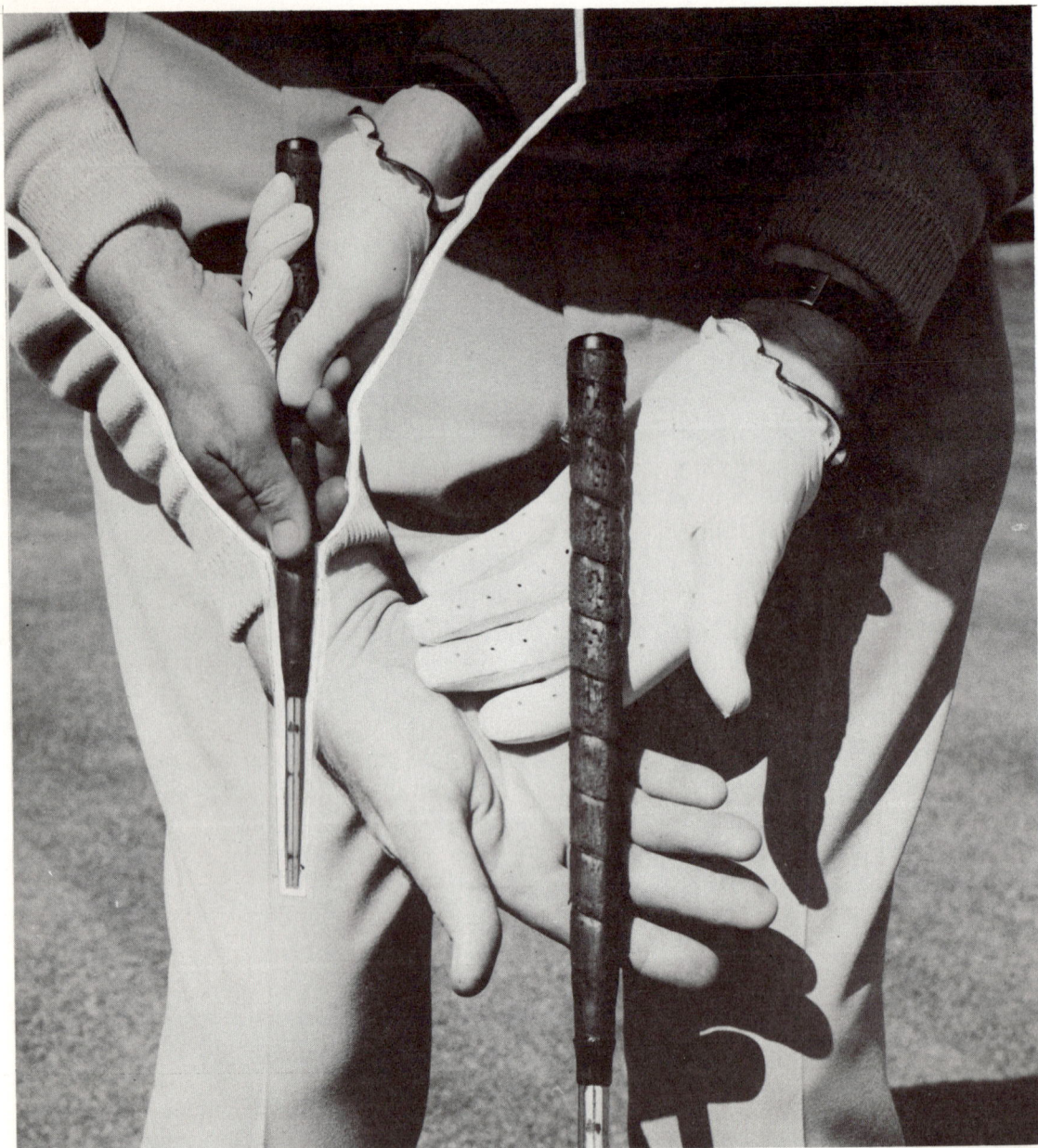

63. In putting we do not want much wrist action, nor do we want an action which is stiff, caused by using arms only. To stop the action being too wristy, grip the putter a little way round the back of the shaft. This gives a movement which incorporates both wrists and arms. After years of experience I find this combination gives the best results.

LOW BACK & THRU

64. Kent player Jennifer Smith, 2 handicap. Whatever stance or pose is adopted it is essential that the putter be kept low to the ground on the backswing and equally low to the ground on the follow-through. Keep the putter blade square to the line throughout the stroke. Obviously if you are faced with a long putt then a longer backswing is required and the putter will leave the ground a little. Practice and experience, through 'feel', will give you this. A good way to judge distance is to place some markers on the green at varying intervals and then putt to each marker in turn. Try to finish level with the marker or just past it.

CHAPTER TWELVE

Bad Shots and How to Cure Them

As golfers we are all seeking perfection. We are rarely, or never, going to find it. But that is what we are chasing.

No matter whether the player is a champion or a beginner, at some point one or more of the problem shots of golf is going to play havoc with his game.

I am going to list some of these troubles – starting with the shot that plagues so many because it is a natural way to hit a golf ball.

The Slice. Some players never conquer this one and learn to live with it. A slice takes place when the swing is out-to-in (the swing path is across the ball from right to left) coupled with the clubface open at impact. This combination is most common.

The ball is given a flat type clockwise spin and usually travels out to the left before curling off to the right. Sometimes it starts straight and then curls off to the right as the forward thrust starts to die. Or it may even start right, then turn right (these variations depending on the swing path of the clubhead at impact). It is the most common fault in golf and almost everybody taking up the game

slices in the early stages. You have to go against nature to effect a cure . . . you cannot beat tuition when starting.

One principal cause is that the player gets his hands and body into the shot too soon, which in turn means that the clubhead is coming in too late. The hands have passed the ball before the clubhead has arrived. The clubhead slides across the ball, which imparts a flat clockwise spin and that curls the ball away to the right.

For a cure make sure that your stance is not too wide, start the club back on an inside path, and try to feel from the top of the backswing that the clubhead is going to get to the ball first – that is, in time. You must also ensure that the clubhead is not going back outside the line of flight and that it is not being picked up too steeply from the ball.

Try to feel that your left shoulder and the clubhead start to turn on the backswing together. Keep the clubface looking at the ball for as long as possible. (See Fig. 47.)

On returning to the ball keep the right shoulder out of the shot – it may help to feel that near the hitting area your hands

Name of Error	Ball Flight	Either Clubhead Path Through Impact Area Is . . .
SLICE	CURVES RIGHT OF TARGET	OUTSIDE TO INSIDE
HOOK	CURVES LEFT OF TARGET	INSIDE TO OUTSIDE
PUSH	STRAIGHT BUT RIGHT OF TARGET	INSIDE TO OUTSIDE
PULL	STRAIGHT BUT LEFT OF TARGET	OUTSIDE TO INSIDE

CORRECT LINE OF FLIGHT
ACTUAL FLIGHT OF BALL
CLUBHEAD PATH

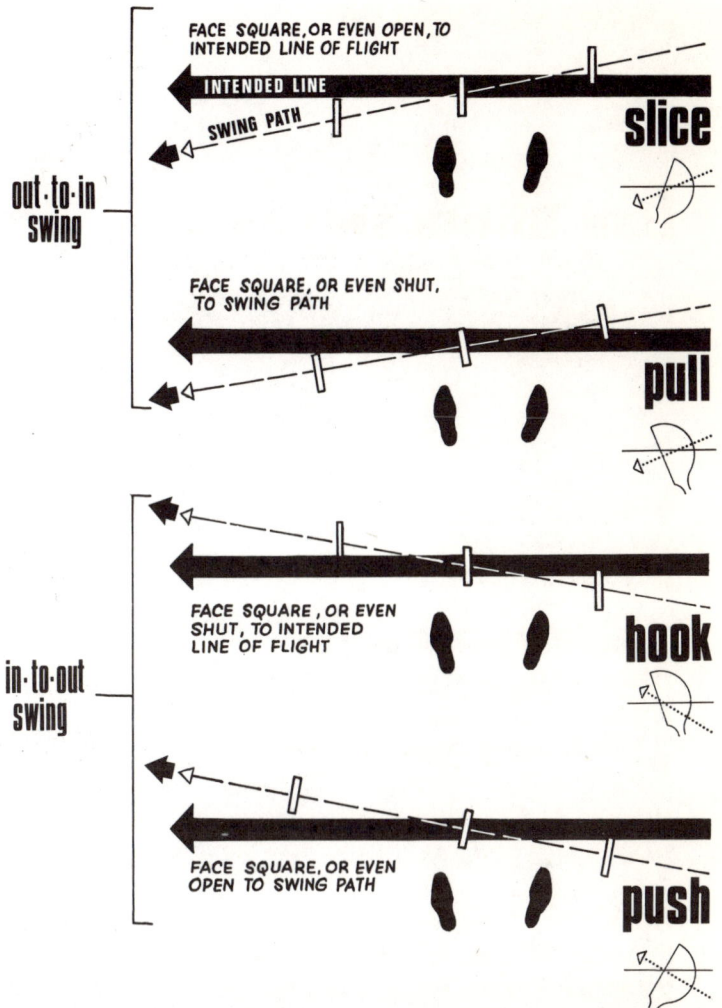

out·to·in swing

FACE SQUARE, OR EVEN OPEN, TO INTENDED LINE OF FLIGHT
INTENDED LINE
SWING PATH
slice

FACE SQUARE, OR EVEN SHUT, TO SWING PATH
pull

in·to·out swing

FACE SQUARE, OR EVEN SHUT, TO INTENDED LINE OF FLIGHT
hook

FACE SQUARE, OR EVEN OPEN TO SWING PATH
push

65. *A general guide to the clubhead swing track* (left) *and ball flight* (right) *for particular shots.*

or right elbow are going to brush past your right-hand trouser pocket.

What you *must not* do is aim off to the left to counter your slice, for that only makes it worse. It is much better to feel you are swinging the clubhead round on the backswing and to the right as you go through. You can even say to yourself 'round and away'.

Otherwise, there are three *'over-corrections'* to try : feel you are going to hit the ball while your back is still facing the target ; feel you are going to hit the ball keeping your right shoulder behind your head ; or put a golf ball box under your left heel. Then try to hit without crushing the box. It stops you turning too soon.

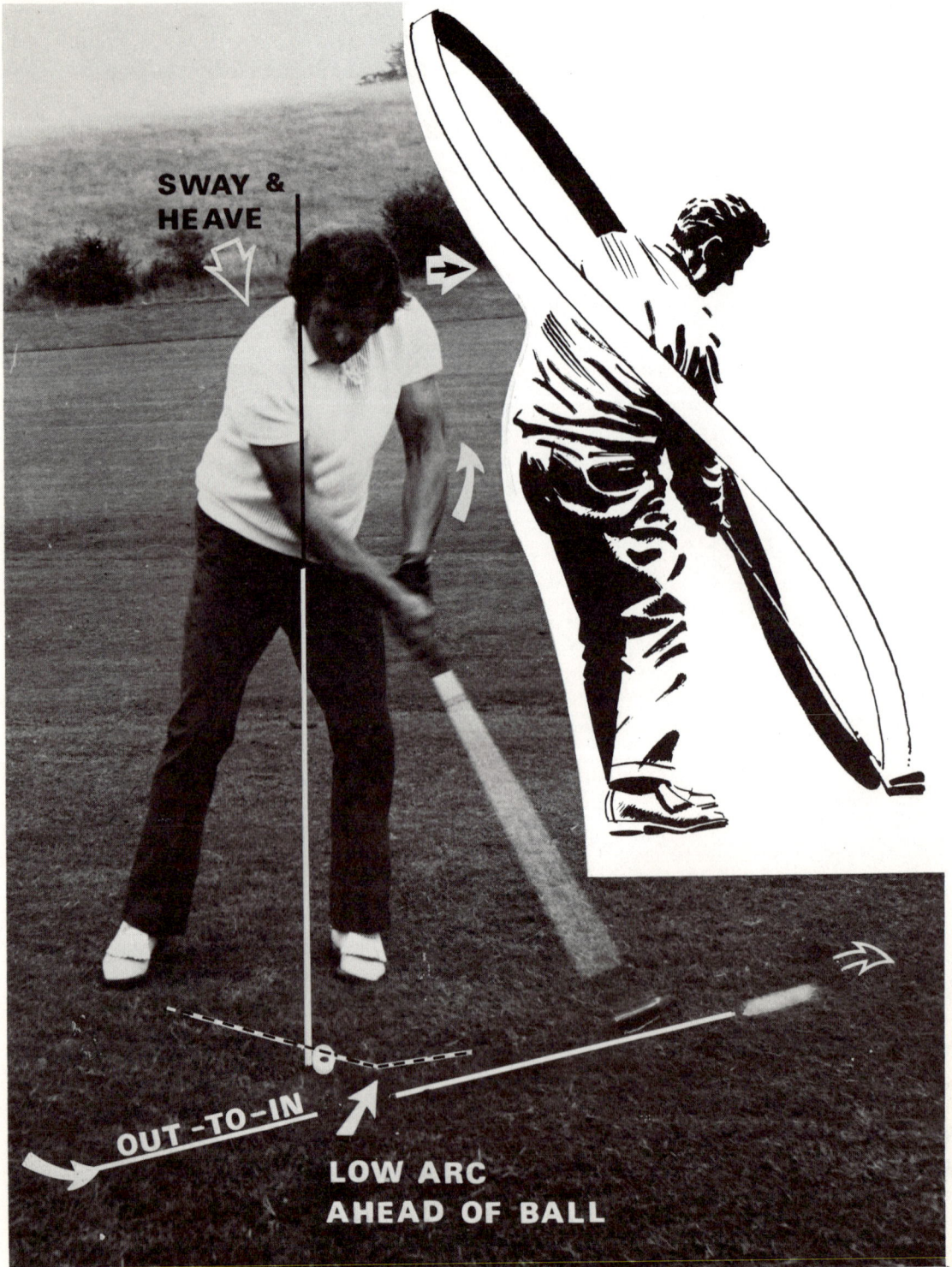

SWAY & HEAVE

OUT-TO-IN

LOW ARC
AHEAD OF BALL

66. (left) *Unfortunately swinging across the ball (from outside-to-in) is the natural way of an untutored swing, and it is not uncommon for the player to sway too. This is known as the beginner's loop — something like swinging round the rim of a crooked wheel, the effect being that the player's body moves in front of the ball before the clubhead arrives. In fact, the clubhead arrives too late, swings round to the left, and if the clubface is open at impact, which it invariably is, the ball starts left and then curves violently to the right. You have to go against nature to effect a cure.*

67. *To get on the right path to cure a slice, imagine you are going to swing the club back and round on an inclined plane to the top of the backswing. From there* make *the clubhead swing through the* ball *to the right of target, something like swinging the clubhead round the rim of a perfect wheel (set on angle to the right). It helps to feel you are going to swing the clubhead past your chin, leaving your head in the same position as it was before the start. Demonstrated here by my 19-year-old, 1 handicap son, Kelvin; in fact his head has recoiled to the right in response to the clubhead swinging through — opposing movements which are nature's way of keeping us in balance. This only happens in a good swing. No change is obvious in the inset picture of Kelvin at 11 years of age.*

RECOIL

No 4 IRON

68. *Jennifer Smith (2 handicap) has kept the right shoulder out of the shot, which is the ideal we are seeking. If the clubhead is swung back to the ball and made to swing to the right of target (an over-correction for the slice) then the right shoulder will go down in response, the left shoulder will go up, and the hips will have turned out of the way. Ultimately, of course, we are seeking a swing from inside-to-straight.*

The Hook. It is said that while poor players slice it takes a good player to hook. The ball starts to the right and then the flat anti-clockwise spin makes the ball turn sharply left as the forward thrust starts to die.

It is quite easy to cure the hook.

The causes can be a flat backswing or the club returning too much on an inside path with the clubface closed; an over-strong grip caused by the right hand being too far under the shaft; a closed clubface; or too steep a backswing producing a loop action from the inside.

If the grip is at fault you already know what the correct grip should be. Check it. (See Figs. 7 and 8.) If the clubface is closing during the downswing to impact, then grip a little firmer with the left hand and ease off with the right.

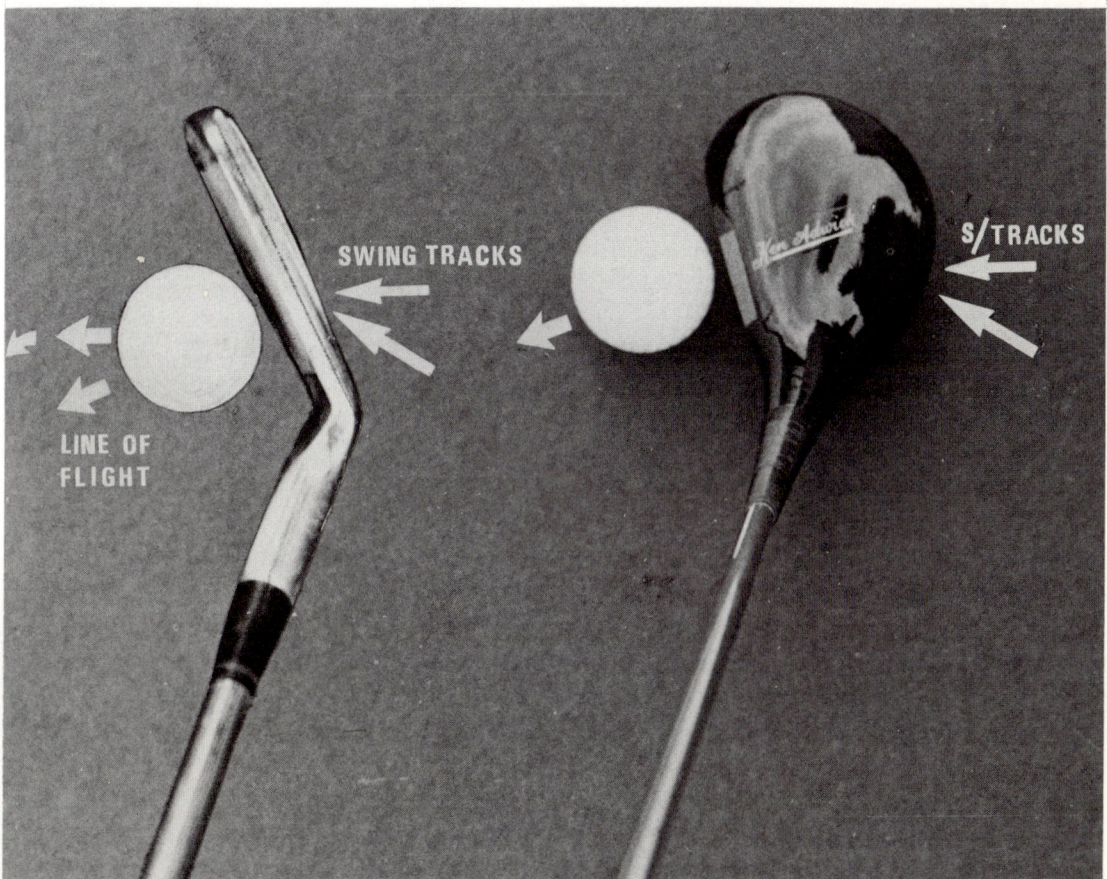

69. *Ideally we all like to hit a shot that starts a little to the right and gently curves on to target. That is the hallmark of a swing on the right lines. However, if those right movements are overdone, a hook is produced with the ball turning sharply to the left, caused by the clubhead being shut at impact. Check your grip. If this is correct and the hook persists, then grip a little firmer with the left hand, and slacken off a little with the right.*

Golf

The Pull. This is the same swing as for the slice, except that the clubhead has returned to the ball square to the swing-line. The ball travels straight left with no side spin. You can blame an out-to-in swing. (See Fig. 65.)

The Push. Same swing as the hook, (inside-to-out) with the difference that the clubface is square to the line it is travelling on. Keep the clubface looking squarely at the ball a little longer on the backswing, and check your grip. (See Fig. 47.) The right hand could have slipped too far on top of the shaft, and the left hand too far under. Or you could be hitting too late, in which case feel the clubhead is going to pass your hands at impact — an over-correction. (See Figs. 19 and 68.)

FACE OPEN TO TARGET LINE

70. *The Push. This is the same swing track as for the hook, but this time the clubface is square to that swing track — that is, open to the intended line of flight. Check your grip, making sure your hands are not in a weak position (too far round to the left). If this is not the case, then your hands at impact are in front of the clubhead. As an over-correction, feel from the top of the backswing that the clubhead is going to arrive at the ball first, or, feel the clubhead is going to pass your hands at impact.*

71. The Skied Shot. This is caused by a narrow, steep backswing through the clubhead leaving the turf too soon. This puts the clubhead in such a position at the top of the backswing that the only movement possible is to swing sharply down into the ball. The hands are in front and the ball is caught off the top of a wooden club. With an iron you are either scooping at impact, or arriving at the ball at impact from out-to-in with the face open. The remedy? Keep the club low to the ground as it sweeps back.

Golf

The Skied Shot. Caused by the ball being hit well above centre of the clubface. The ball flies high rather than long.

This error is usually brought about by picking the club up steeply rather than swinging the clubhead back low. So to cure it try sweeping the club back low to the ground at the start of the backswing for about 15 inches — just brushing the turf as the clubhead swings round and up on an inclined plane.

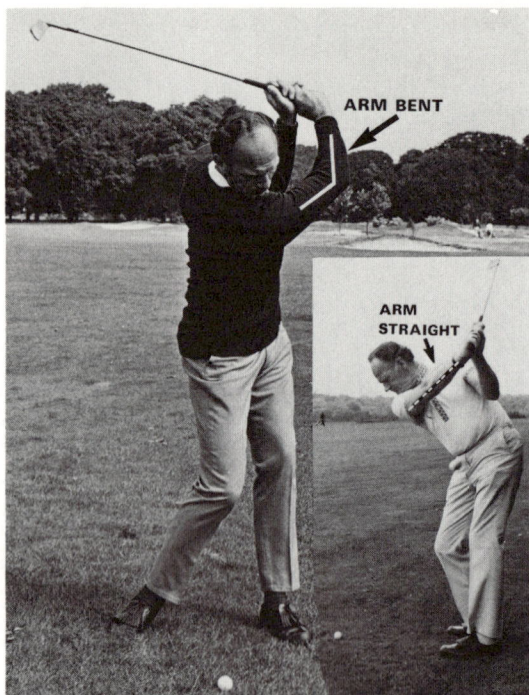

The Topped Shot. The ball is hit above centre and top spin imparted. This means it will travel in the direction it has been struck but will never leave the ground.

Keeping your eye on the ball while swinging helps. 'Head up' is one of the causes. The main one, however, is swaying into the shot either on backswing or downswing. So stand still and make sure there is no body swaying movement. Don't stoop too much at address, and make sure you keep your head behind the ball until the clubhead has passed. Hit past your chin. Bent arms through impact are another cause as is trying to scoop the ball into the air.

73. *He has kept his arm bent at impact and would have topped the shot had he not lowered his body to compensate.*

82

72. (facing page) *Our 'Enery, otherwise former boxing champion Henry Cooper, is seen playing left-handed. At the top of his backswing his right arm is bent. This is not a crime in itself but it would have been better had it been a little straighter.*

The Heavy Shot. This is where you hit turf before hitting the ball — a chopping action. The cause is much the same as for a skied shot, although you may be swinging even steeper.

74. *A lady amateur who has topped a shot through both arms being bent at impact. Professional Graham Marsh, an Australian, shows how it should be done with the letter 'Y' maintained through the shot.*

75. *Here I am deliberately hitting steeply into the ball and taking turf before impact. We call this hitting heavy. If you are hitting the ground first, the answer is to sweep the clubhead back low and on a wide arc, and low through the shot. Also avoid chopping down on the ball from the top of the backswing.*

The answer is to keep the clubhead low to the ground — say for 15 inches when starting the backswing as it sweeps round on an inclined plane — and stay on that path. This will stop any dip or sway.

The Shank. It is a dreadful moment when you get an attack of the shanks. The ball flies off at right angles and you will find a ball mark appears at the heel of the club. Pushing at the ball with an exaggerated in-to-out swing path is the common error.

Shanking can occur with any iron — more usually with the 8- or 9-irons, wedge and sand iron. What happens is the ball is struck with the heel of the club. There are three causes, two of which are rare. The most common is through rushing at the ball with an exaggerated in-to-out swing path — a stiff-wristed action. This type is the one I am going to outline.

Check your grip, stand your normal distance from the ball, keep the clubface square at address and throughout the backswing, and as an over-correction feel you are swinging the club a little on an outside line on the backswing while keeping the clubhead as low as possible when swinging back and through.

Feel that if anything the clubhead is travelling across the line of flight. You can also try holding the club a little further down the grip. Do not push the clubhead back and through — swing it backwards and forwards and be relaxed. (See Fig. 27.)

The Smother. This is allied to the hook. The ball flies low, usually turning to the left.

It is produced by a hooded and shut clubface at impact, and the usual cause is the grip. (See Figs. 7 and 8.) The right hand is in a too powerful position under the shaft and the clubhead turns over at impact. Make sure that the 'V's of your hands point up the shaft, as you see it from your own view point.

You can also smother the shot by turning your body into the ball. This is allied to the pull. (See Figs. 41 and 42.)

76. The Shank. Caused by a stiff action through the ball (on an exaggerated inside-to-out track). Due to the wrists being too stiff, the clubhead is not released and is pushed into the ball, striking it with the neck of the club. It is similar to a defensive prod at cricket. The hands are leading the clubhead. The cure, an over-correction, is to make the clubhead get to the ball first, or feel you are swinging across the ball from out-to-in. This will neutralise all the undesirable actions. Anxiety is usually a prime factor in the shank.

HANDS
LEADING
CLUBHEAD

SHANK

TO
TARGET

CLUBHEAD
PATH

SHANK

CHAPTER THIRTEEN

The Common Awkward Lies – Playing in Wind – Some General Advice

Now you have a basic guide to how to play golf. What I want to do next is to touch briefly on some special points giving a summary of what you should be remembering when you play the game.

When you have a *downhill* lie then play the ball from the middle of the feet or a little right of centre. You can take one less club than you would normally use for that distance. If the shot seems a 6-iron then take a 7-iron. Be careful not to come off the ball too soon.

77. The Downhill Shot. Position yourself so the ball is a little right of centre. Use a club one less powerful than would seem required – that is, instead of a 7-iron take an 8-iron. It is essential to stay down on the shot, and follow the slope of the ground with the clubhead. You will find more weight on the left foot than the right.

An *uphill* lie is easier. Play the ball from a little left of centre and expect the ball to be high flying. So choose a club one or two bigger than seems indicated. That is a 7- or 8-iron, for example, when a 9-iron would be used on the flat. Don't fall back at impact.

A restricted swing for both these lies is advisable.

When standing above the ball the likelihood is that the ball will slice to the right. Make sure you aim off a little to the left. Position yourself so the ball is almost opposite your left heel, with your weight back on the heels. When swinging the club feel you are following the surface of the ground.

78. *An Uphill Lie. Address the ball so it is just inside the left heel. Your weight will be more on your right foot, with the right leg straighter than the left. This time select a club which is more powerful than would seem indicated – that is, a 3- or 4-iron instead of a 5-iron. From this lie you will experience a higher flying shot. Once again swing with the line of the slope.*

79. *Standing Above The Ball. This is one of the most awkward lies in golf and invariably a slice will result. Address the ball with the weight towards the heels and have it positioned off the left heel. As a slice is likely, aim off to the left, but this depends on the club used. Aim off more for a powerful iron than a shorter club. The backswing is automatically steeper but try to keep it as low to the ground as possible.*

Golf

If standing below the ball the tendency is to hook the shot to the left. To counteract this, aim a little right of target. Hold the club an inch or two down the grip with the ball positioned just left of centre. It does help to keep your hands a little in front of the ball at address and feel they are in that position again at impact. Once again, follow the contour of the ground with the clubhead – or feel that you are.

When behind a tree settle for a chip out sideways unless there is an excellent chance, if you are far enough back, to play over the top of the tree. Don't try bending the ball round. Leave that to the experts.

When facing a narrow fairway where accuracy is essential, play the percentage shot. You can go down the grip of your driver, but settle for a 3-wood or long iron and loss of distance.

Avoid the temptation to steer the ball. Stand still, keep your eye on the back of the ball, and trust your swing.

If the grass is wet then you must try to hit the ball first.

Should it be windy then widen your stance at address to help with balance. When against the wind play the ball a little further back towards your right foot than normal, and keep the clubhead low to the ground on the backswing and after impact. If the wind is with you, position the ball just inside the left heel. With a sidewind aim off and let the wind bring the ball back on line. Don't fight it.

Don't get anxious and start to play unduly safe if you are scoring well. You must play positively from the first shot.

Sensible optimism is the policy. Don't get over confident or despondent. The game of golf consists not of what has just happened but of the shot about to be played.

You will probably feel extra nervous on the first tee where other players may be watching you drive off. That is a testing moment for all of us golfers. Rather than react to the outsiders, look long and hard at the ball, concentrate on the clubhead and feel you are swinging at an even pace. Remind yourself how often you have played off that tee safely.

As for judging which club is required for a particular distance, that can only be learned with experience. To generalise, it is better to be past the pin rather than short. A good tip is to play for the top of the flagstick when within range.

Finally, here is a summary of some important basics that will help you to get good results :

Check your grip.

Make sure your stance and alignment are correct.

During the swing think only of the clubhead and the path you have been taught to swing it on. If your swing shape is right the correct body movements come automatically.

Keep your head still.

Don't hit at the ball, hit through it.

You need effortless power, not powerful effort. It is not how hard you swing, rather how you swing it hard.

The swing is one continuous unbroken movement from start to finish. Keep those heavy body muscles out. Swing the clubhead and make the hands deliver the power.

80. *Standing Below The Ball. Here the tendency is to hook the shot, so aim off correspondingly to the right. Position the ball just left of centre, keep your hands a little in front of the ball at address, and as you will swing flat, feel that you are going to swing more upright. It helps to hold the club a little way down the grip.*

81. *The most photographed position in golf. Do not try to copy it because you will only overdo what is going to happen naturally anyway. The golfer is Bruce Devlin of Australia, and he has the expertise to get the clubhead to the ball in time. It requires a lightning whip action. Note the right shoulder has been kept back and out of the way, the left hip has moved out of the way too (a twistlike action between shoulder and hip), and although his head has kept back behind the ball his knees have moved towards the target. Repeat, don't try to do this, it is a natural response to the swinging of the clubhead on the proper path.*

82.   Better to have Ryder Cup golfer Clive Clark's position in mind. The clubhead arrives in time. The body reaction to this swing thought is that the right shoulder is kept back, the left shoulder has gone up, and the left hip has turned considerably. More important, though, the clubhead will not arrive late at impact. Always feel that the clubhead is going to arrive first.

CHAPTER FOURTEEN

Exercises for Better Golf

Don't fall into the trap of thinking you have to build up body muscles like a Mr Universe in order to hit a ball far and true. Hitting golf balls, obviously with the correct swing in mind, is the best exercise I know to build the right *golfing* muscles.

However, as the hands are the only link between you and the club (a chain is only as strong as its weakest link) it is essential that they are strong enough to deliver the power generated by the body in the form of speed and also to maintain control over the clubhead.

Should a player be a strong individual, yet weak in the hands, then they will act like a resistor in an electric circuit and will be unable to deliver the power. This is why a slightly built player with strong hands can very often outdrive a seemingly powerfully built player whose hands are weak in comparison with his physique.

The best way to strengthen the hands and forearms is to knead a rubber ball that fits into the palm of the hand, or to use various spring devices which are readily available on the market. If you work diligently at these exercises you will be pleasantly surprised by the results.

Strength in the legs is also beneficial. A boa constrictor has to have its tail curled round a firm object in order to exert its strength. In golf, the legs, together with well anchored feet, act in a similar fashion. Any exercise which helps to strengthen the legs will add to consistency with shot making. Hitting golf balls with feet together and knees flexed will contribute to this.

Swing thoughts

As we are all individuals we naturally think in different ways. . . . It follows then that there is more than one correct swing thought of how to hit a golf ball, but they all amount to the same thing. For example, should you find hitting through the ball or making the clubhead catch up with the hands at impact difficult to feel, then have the thought of swinging the clubface against the ball – *not at it*. By thinking this way you will still get your maximum clubhead speed at impact which in turn will take you automatically to a complete follow-through.

This is a different thought, yet the end result will be the same.

Practice

There is no substitute for practice if a player wishes to improve, and there is no use in practising aimlessly. It *must* be

92

When practising what you have been told I suggest you start by using one of the shorter clubs – 5-, 6- or 7-iron, as they are much easier to control. When you feel you have mastered the fault, only then should the longer clubs be used.

When practising through the clubs, always start with the short irons, playing more shots with these and gradually lessening the number with each club as you go through the bag.

Possibly by the time the driver is ready for its turn you may have tired a little, so it is advisable to play only a few shots with this club as there is a danger of starting to slog or heave at the ball.

83. Another swing thought – swinging the clubface squarely up against the ball. This thought will also help to stop swaying in the direction of the target before impact.

done intelligently with something in mind, always to a target, not just hitting golf balls in any old direction.

Should you have a fault to eradicate, first have a lesson or two from your professional and then you will know what to practise.

CHAPTER FIFTEEN

Etiquette – Explanations of Some Golfing Terms

To conclude, here is some guidance on the important subject of etiquette. You will be judged as much on how you behave around the course as on the standard of your play.

Read these simple rules carefully and try to behave as indicated.

I have followed these with a description of some basic golf terms.

Good luck with your golf and I wish you speedy progress. Please say hello should we meet.

Etiquette on the course is very important and must be observed out of respect to others playing, and to the course itself.

Do not move, talk or stand near to the person about to play his shot. Stand opposite the player not nearer than, say, 15 feet . . . distraction can ruin a shot.

Do not play until the golfers in front are well out of range. A golf ball can inflict severe injury. Should your ball go in the direction of another player or bystander, shout the golfer's warning cry, 'Fore'.

In the interest of others, play without undue delay. Be ready to play when your turn comes. Prior to putting, park your trolley at the back of the green or in the direction of the next tee. Always leave the green immediately the hole has been completed as this helps the flow of play. Don't mark your score card on the green.

Always call faster players through. After you have signalled them on never continue playing until they have completed the hole.

Always watch your ball until it has come to rest. Should it go into trouble, such as long grass or bushes, mark the landing spot carefully, which helps to avoid undue delay.

When leaving a bunker, smooth out the marks you have made in the sand. Remember the players following who may visit the same trap. Leave the bunker as you would expect to find it.

Replace and press down turf (divots) you may have taken during the shot. Always repair your pitch marks on the green, not only for the benefit of players following but also to help preserve the condition of the course.

Do not drop but place the flagstick on the green. Always centre the pin before dropping it into the hole, then there is no danger of damaging the lip round the cup. *Never* put your bag of clubs on the green or wheel your caddy car across it.

These simple rules of etiquette serve the following main purposes:

To reduce the possibility of injury to yourself and others on the course.
To speed up play.

To sustain the enjoyment of the game not only for yourself but all concerned.

You will be judged by your golfing etiquette as much as by your play.

Some Golfing Terms

Address: Taking up a stance and grounding the club (except in a hazard) prior to making a swing.
Approach Shot: A shot to the putting surface or green.
Apron: The area immediately surrounding the putting area.
Away: The ball furthest away from the green, or the pin when on the green. Should be played first.
Birdie: One stroke under the nominated par of the hole.
Bogey: One stroke above the nominated par of the hole.
Bogey (Double Bogey):   Two strokes above the nominated par of the hole.
Bunker: 'A hazard, usually filled with sand.
Casual Water: An area temporarily covered by water.
Divot: Turf removed or displaced by a player's club during the swing.
Dog-Leg: A hole where the fairway bends quite sharply to the left or right, before reaching the green or putting surface.
Down (Match Play):   The number of holes a player is behind his opponent.
Eagle: Two strokes below the nominated par for the hole.
Fairway: The closely mown surface of play between the teeing area and green.
Fore: A warning cry to any person in the way of play.
Green: The specially prepared surface, closely mown, where only a putter should be used.
Gross Score: The total number of strokes taken before a player's handicap is deducted.
Halved: A term used to indicate identical scores at a hole in match play.
Handicap: Strokes given according to the player's ability at golf. Usually calculated on the player's best score.

Golf

Hazard: Designated bunker, sand trap, or any water area put there to catch a wayward shot.

Honour: The right to tee off first, earned by the player scoring the lowest on the preceding hole.

Hook: A shot played by a right-handed player which turns to the left during its flight. For the left-hander the ball turns to the right.

Lie: The stationary position of the ball after it has been played. The same term is used relating to the angle of the shaft to the clubhead, when the sole of the club is placed on the ground at address.

Marker (a): A small coin or round plastic disc used to mark the ball on the green if it has to be lifted for any reason.

Marker (b): Tee markers defining the forward limits of the teeing area. Marker posts to play for if the green is not visible, or to mark out-of-bounds boundaries. . . . A person marking a player's card.

Match Play: A type of competition in which each hole is a separate contest. The winner is the player or side that wins more holes than there are left to play . . . Example, 3 holes up with only 2 to play.

Net Score: The number of shots played less the handicap.

Obstruction: An artificial object erected, placed or left on the course.

Par: A number of shots a player should take for the hole according to the yardage, this to include two putts per green . . . i.e. Par 3 up to 250 yards, Par 4 between 251 and 475 yards, Par 5, 476 yards and over.

Press: To attempt to hit beyond one's natural power.

Provisional Ball: A second ball played if the player is in doubt about the first one being out-of-bounds or lost.

Pull: A ball hit straight left of target. For the left-hander the flight would be straight right.

Push: A ball hit straight right of target. For the left-hander, straight left.

Rough: Areas of the course covered with long grass.

Rough (Semi): Areas covered with grass which is longer than the fairways. These areas are adjacent to the tee, fairways, green or hazards.

Rub of the Green: A term used when a ball is stopped or deflected by an outside agency when the ball is in motion.

Slice: A shot which when played by a right-handed player turns to the right during flight. A shot which starts left, then turns right during flight is the most common. Opposite directions for the left-hander.

S.S.S.: Standard Scratch Score. A score in which a scratch player is expected to go round the course playing from medal tees in summer conditions.

Stance: Position of the feet and body when addressing the ball.

Stroke: Any forward motion of the clubhead made with the intention of striking the ball.

Stroke Play (Medal Play): A competition based on the total number of strokes taken for the round.

Tee: A peg on which the ball is elevated above the ground in preparation for the ball being hit off the teeing area.

Top: When the ball is hit above its centre, imparting clockwise spin.

Up: In match play, the number of holes a player is in advance of his opponent.